Challenging the Classroom Standard Through Museum-Based Education

School in the Park

Challenging the Classroom Standard Through Museum-Based Education

School in the Park

Edited by

Ian Pumpian
Douglas Fisher
Susan Wachowiak
City Heights Educational Collaborative

Routledge
Taylor & Francis Group
New York London

First published by Lawrence Erlbaum Associates, Inc., Publishers
10 Industrial Avenue
Mahwah, New Jersey 07430

Transferred to digital printing 2010 by Routledge

Routledge

270 Madison Avenue
New York, NY 10016

2 Park Square, Milton Park
Abingdon, Oxon OX14 4RN, UK

Cover design by Tomai Maridou

Library of Congress Cataloging-in-Publication Data

Challenging the classroom standard through museum-based education :
   school in the park / [edited by] Ian Pumpian, Douglas Fisher,
   and Susan Wachowiak.
       p. cm.
   Includes bibliographical references and index.
   ISBN 0-8058-5635-8 (c. : alk. paper)
   ISBN 0-8058-5636-6 (pbk. : alk. paper)
     1. Museums and schools—United States.   2. School field trips—United States.
   3. Museums—Educational aspects—United States.   I. Pumpian, Ian.
   II. Fisher, Douglas, 1965–   III. Wachowiak, Susan.

LB1047.C52   2005
371.3'84—dc22   2005040101
                                                                      CIP

Contents

Foreword   vii
George E. Hein

Preface   xi

Acknowledgments   xiii

2004–2005 School in the Park Teachers
and Museum Educators   xvii

1   School in the Park—A Unique Learning Experience
for Children and Teachers   1
Ian Pumpian, Susan Wachowiak, and Douglas Fisher

2   Perspectives on Learning—Creating Optimal Conditions
for Learning   15
Ian Pumpian, Maria Grant, and Susan Wachowiak

3   Talking in Museums: When Vices Turn Into Virtues
Exploring Oral Language Development   29
Diane Lapp and James Flood

4	Reading in the Park *Nancy Frey*	43
5	An Authentic Context for Writing to Learn and Teaching Writing Intentionally *Leif Fearn and Nancy Farnan*	61
6	Arts as a Centerpiece for Integrated Learning *Nan L. McDonald*	79
7	Where Is the Mathematics? Everywhere! *Kate Masarik*	97
8	The Opportunity to Learn Science Like Scientists: Museums Are a Good Idea *Donna Ross*	109
9	Engaging Students in Social Studies Through Exploration, Documentation, and Analysis: Museums and Field Studies Can Bring Social Studies to Life *Emily M. Schell*	123

About the Editors	147
About the Authors	149
Author Index	153
Subject Index	157

Foreword

George E. Hein
Lesley University

Public museums and public schools share both a parallel and an interactive history. Both derive from 18th century enlightenment concepts of educating the general public. Emerging nationalist governments began to take responsibility for the welfare of all their citizens and education was acknowledged as both a necessity and a benefit to society. But how such education for the masses was to be provided was not at all clear. And because childhood itself, as a discrete human condition, is a modern social invention, it was not evident that childhood was the most appropriate time for publicly supported enculturation.

Two kinds of educational institutions that emerged from these developing nationalist, populist (and modern imperialist) trends were the public museum and the public school. But as even children worked, traditionally within the family and later in factories and other commercial establishments, schooling for the masses was limited to a few early years or for a few hours after long workdays. Likewise, 19th century museums had limited open hours, often with restrictions on attendance, and provided few opportunities for connections to the schools. In the last half of the 19th century school attendance, at least for a few years, became mandatory, and schools surpassed museums as the primary agents for socialization and formal education.

But museums, although marginalized as major educational institutions, continued to play a role in public education and transmission of culture and also continued to expand. The 20th century has seen an incredible surge of museum growth. Children's museums and science centers are totally modern inventions, and the current thriving art and history museums, not to mention aquaria, zoos, botanical gardens, and so on, were unimaginable only a few generations ago.

Early museums clearly viewed themselves as educational institutions, although the connection to public schools was tenuous. During the progressive era, in the late 19th and early 20th centuries, as schools adopted more experiential, inquiry-based, and object-centered pedagogies, they became themselves more museum-like and many developed close ties with museums. The St. Louis public schools had a famous museum service that provided object kits to schools; the younger children at the Dewey Laboratory School in Chicago visited the Columbian Field Museum for an hour and a half every week; and progressive schools had children do projects that resembled museum-style exhibits. Pictures of children's weaving activities in John Cotton Dana's Newark museum illustrate activities similar to those at the Dewey Laboratory School. They also strikingly resemble what happens at such current museums as the Tsongas History Center in Lowell, Massachusetts.

The decline of progressive education in the mid-20th century resulted in decreased museum–school connections and reversion to more traditional field trips. Intense school–museum relationships have waxed and waned ever since, reflecting social funding priorities. Like all progressive educational practices, they have a long continuous history, but have never reached more than minority status in public education.

What all the museum–school connections share now, and have through their history, is a commitment to progressive education practices. They recognize that education should begin with experience—with doing and interpreting objects. But progressive education has a broader agenda: the raw material of experience needs to be developed, studied, and interpreted to develop deeper understanding; in short, to learn. Experience is educative, as Dewey said long ago, but education is the result of becoming engaged with the problematic outcomes of reflecting on experience (i.e., inquiring) in order to understand the meaning of the experiences. In addition, the progressive education agenda includes a powerful social component: Education should support participatory democracy; it should reflect the democratic society we strive to achieve.

The latest upsurge of museum–school partnerships is now about 15 years old. It grew out of a maturing movement in the school community to make school activities reflect the growing research-based understanding of the sociocultural components of learning. Simultaneously, museum educators increasingly understood that such ideas, based on the work of Dewey, Piaget, and Vygotsky, also applied to their programs. The museum–school movement first came to the attention of the wider museum education community in the 1990s with the publication of proceedings from a conference in Minneapolis in 1995 followed by the Smithsonian Institution's *True Needs, True Partners* (1996). The range of connections between schools and museums is broad, from close collaborations between one museum and one school to schools established within museums and partnerships between multiple schools and museums. More recently, this whole approach, as well as the specific school–museum partnerships, has struggled to survive as formal education once again moves away from progressive ideas to more authoritarian structures, more test-driven assignments and less leeway for individual teachers to shape curriculum. The federal No Child Left Behind legislation and its heavy, mandated emphasis on testing and accountability (narrowly defined) does not appear conducive to school–museum partnerships.

One of the largest and most extensive of these school–museum partnerships is the School in the Park in San Diego. Not only does it involve 10 museums, all located within culturally rich Balboa Park in San Diego, but it now also includes 800 children, all fourth, fifth, and sixth graders from one large inner-city elementary school. Perhaps most important, the program staff and teachers have struggled to reconcile their Dewey-like progressive goals and practices with the mandates of current California school curriculum and testing requirements. This volume not only describes the School in the Park activities—how children spend a week a month in selected museums, incorporating their museum work into their curriculum—it also describes in detail how these activities are designed to match the state curriculum and how they address each of the traditional subjects from language arts to science. Most encouraging, early results from mandated tests suggest that the partnership is successful in helping students succeed in school, enjoy their work, and improve their performances.

Public schools currently face enormous difficulties. They struggle in the face of decreasing public support—both financial and moral—to educate all of our society's diverse students, while they grapple with increased poverty, decreased social services, and overwhelming administrative pressures. All efforts to break out of this difficult situation that makes failure so easy require an enormous marshalling of resources, huge amounts of work, and strong, dedicated staff with faith and vision. It's clear from the descriptions in this volume that School in the Park, with its generous support from Price Charities, its strong staff, and additional collaboration with educators from San Diego State University, has recognized the enormity of the problems and addressed them with the forces needed. This book tells wonderful stories of the children, how they are learning and how each component of the school curriculum is addressed through the collaboration with a range of museums. I can only hope that a subsequent volume will report continuing academic success and will provide equally compelling and detailed description of the complex organization and intense staff commitment that makes this project possible.

REFERENCE

Frankel, D. B. (1996). *True needs, true partners: Museums and schools transforming education*. Washington, DC: Smithsonian Institution.

Preface

> *Where there is life, there are already eager and impassioned activities. Growth is not something done to them [students]; it is something they do... Until the democratic criterion of the intrinsic significance of every growing experience is recognized we shall be intellectually confused by the demand for adaptation to external aims.*
> —Dewey (1916, p. 42)

All those interested in and charged with educating children will find this book useful in exploring powerful learning experiences that occur outside traditional classroom settings. With an increased focus on accountability and achievement, less attention and importance is being given to field trips and other community-based learning experiences. People associated with School in the Park posit that "formal" learning can be supported and enhanced through extended community-based "informal" learning experiences. The purpose of this book is to demonstrate the viability of merging formal and informal learning in School in the Park as a means of gaining further insight into effective education. By examining this approach to educating children, we believe readers will discover the value of using nontraditional settings as extensions of their classrooms. When done correctly this student engagement is enhanced, a depth of understanding is achieved, and more professionals become part of the learning process.

In the chapters that follow, we present the significant themes and connections that are emerging within School in the Park. School in the Park is analyzed by various stakeholders in order to provide a sense of the instructional design of the program as well as how teaching and learning in various content areas are operationalized. In the words of Sol Price, celebrated businessman and philanthropist who provided the inspiration and substantial resources for School in the Park, it is important to describe how the program impacts the *"character, confidence, and competence"* of those involved.

Our intent is to provide the story of School in the Park both as information for those interested in expanding traditional education programs to include larger community-based settings and as a tribute to those who continue in the dedicated pursuit of making School in the Park a program that improves educational outcomes for children. Every community has exciting places that could naturally be used as places in which standards could be well taught and deeply learned. Each school has the capacity to establish relationships outside the traditional school to regularly access these unused natural classrooms. It is our hope that this book will enhance the reader's prior knowledge such that those potential community-based classrooms are used to impact the *"character, confidence, and competence"* of more students. These are the circumstances from which School in the Park commenced. The evolution, the journey, and the resulting story are truly phenomenal.

Acknowledgments

This book and the program behind it could not exist without the dedication and determination of many people. The enthusiasm we all had in the first year of the City Heights Educational Collaborative was quickly dampened. We entered a school that had been built one year earlier to house 900 students only find over 1,400 enrolled. Portables and prefabricated units were being placed on what had been carefully planned open spaces. Four classrooms were located in the multipurpose room separated by cafeteria tables. A class of second graders was being bussed to the middle school and five kindergarten classrooms were housing 12 a.m./p.m. classes. The morale and patience of the staff and families was being tested and the educational experience we wanted to provide these youngsters was being threatened.

School in the Park was created in this climate. It is arguably one of the nation's most exciting large-scale innovations. It was designed and implemented to respond to our space crisis by investing in, and not compromising, educational practice. It was designed and implemented because people were creative, willing to take a risk, and fully dedicated to providing 1,480 children from the community of City Heights a quality education. And it still is.

Sol Price is among the nation's most celebrated businessmen and philanthropists. The San Diego community has prospered from his leadership, entrepreneurship, and giving. It was Sol Price who one day proposed the idea of having one quarter of the school's students in the museums of Balboa Park as a means of dealing with the fact that the school was one quarter over-enrolled. Who can forget his first question on the subject, "Can you teach a student to read in the art museum or at the zoo?"

Sol and his son Robert Price have brought the resources, influence, and know-how of their family charity to the School in the Park. Robert knows the operation inside and out and has held high standards for the program's management and innovation. He has assigned his key staff to maintain even closer contact with the museums and institutes. Heidi Gantwerk and Ann Bossler have made School in the Park what it is today.

San Diego State University President Stephen Weber, Associate Vice President Ethan Singer, and Dean Skip Meno have made our fine university's partnership in City Heights a source of pride and joy and central to our work as an engaged university. We appreciate the numerous SDSU faculty, many of whom contributed chapters to this volume, who have made School in the Park part of their research and teaching. They have further validated our efforts and presented us new challenges. Similarly, SDSU project staff Mike Corke, Lorri Frangkiser, Lannie Kanefski, and Steve Spencer have helped us quantify and qualify what School in the Park is.

Each museum director, educational coordinator, and educational specialist has integrated School in the Park into their institutions. They have treasured this program and nurtured it as part of their precious collections. They are the caretakers of our collective culture and unite the past with the future.

Early in our partnership, the idea of School in the Park was "pitched" to teachers. Already overwhelmed and opening a new and overcrowded school, many were quite prepared to dismiss us, and the "idea." But not Loretta Saez. This teacher was the first to see the possibility and she urged her peers not to dismiss the possibility too quickly. She gained the support of the teachers and later came to be the first teacher on special assignment in the park. Since then, Linda Feldman has aptly functioned in and expanded that role.

When the teachers bought in, they really bought in! Their energy, talent, and commitment to their students and the greatness of this program is its beginning and end. The Rosa Parks professional development team—Aida Allen, Maureen Begley, Donna Kopenski, Kelly Moore, Sheryl Segal, and Elizabeth Soriano—have extended themselves in significant ways to ensure all teachers had access to quality support.

Of course, a program like this demands leadership. Emilee Watts, the founding principal of Rosa Parks Elementary School, had the will and skill to negotiate and guide the teachers, the institutions, the families, the partners, and the logistics. As the interim principal, Barbara Bethel has dedicated herself to further align the curriculum offered in School in the Park. She understands the balance and demands of formal and informal education. Their administrative team, especially Rick De La Pena, has made an amazingly complicated program appear seamless to students, families, and staffs.

And of course we acknowledge the 800+ students who attend School in the Park each year and teach us that we must never limit our expectations of them. They remind us each day that we can and must provide them the very best, for they are the very best.

Finally, Susan Wachowiak, fellow editor, is the heart and soul of School in the Park. She is our leader, our cheerleader, and our natural resource.

REFERENCE

Dewey, J. (1916). *Democracy and education.* New York: The Free Press.

2004–2005 School in the Park Teachers

Alexandria Allen
Kate Andersen-Grey
Sue Barnett
Mario Borayo
Colleen Crandall
Roberta Dawson
Audrey Day
Adrienne Feistal
Andrea Fiske
Bob Ford
Marcus Greene
Monica Gutierrez
Laura Harriman
Joan Jones

Marilin Levitan
Veronica Lias
James Lyons
Shayne McCool
Autumn Miller
Patty Osborne
Monica Perez
Khan Pham
Romana Ayala Reed
Juan Robles
Carrier Smith
Melinda Tanasescu
Rachel Tuttle
Carlie Ward
Diana Yemha

2004–2005 MUSEUM EDUCATORS

Hall of Champions—Kitty Smith
Junior Theater—Bryn Fillers and Graham Russo
Museum of Photographic Arts—Vivian Kung Haga, Chantal Legro, and Nora Shields

Reuben H. Fleet Science Center—Colleen Pelak
San Diego Aerospace Museum—Brian Canfield, Bill Fox, and Roscoe Davis
San Diego Museum of Art—Karin Baker and Aira Burgos
San Diego Museum of History—Kim Vukasovich and Rebecca Lawrence
San Diego Museum of Man—Eric Mason
San Diego Natural History Museum—Susan Cobb
San Diego Zoo—Judi Bowes

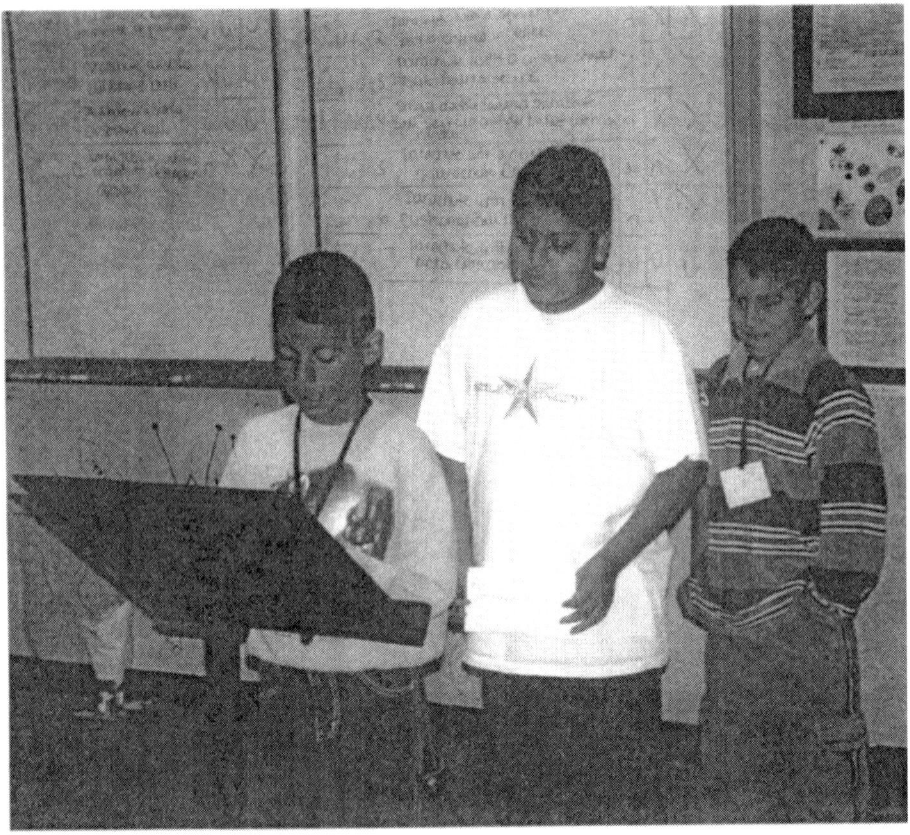

CHAPTER ONE

School in the Park—
A Unique Learning Experience
for Children and Teachers

Ian Pumpian
Susan Wachowiak
Douglas Fisher

We believe School in the Park is a unique and bold educational endeavor implemented during a time of shrinking education budgets. Few schools and districts may have access to the resources necessary to operate a program on the scale of School in the Park. However, the practical lessons learned are useful for understanding how community-based learning experiences can enhance educational outcomes for children. In addition, conditions can be created in which students will be motivated, focused, and excited about engaging in challenging learning tasks that most would consider out of their reach.

Provided the right conditions exist, we would be thrilled if this book facilitated every school being able to offer multiple opportunities to apply the principles of School in the Park. At the very least, understanding the principles and practices of School in the Park will result in rethinking and reorganizing traditional field trip resources and moving instruction beyond (see Fig. 1.1).

These principles and practices are described and exemplified throughout this book. We also hope that this book prompts new public and private interest in creating partnerships that continue to promote adding new environments and experiences to excite and enhance learning outcomes for students. Readers are challenged to begin to create their own asset maps of facilities and locations in their immediate community that are readily available to provide educational opportunities that will extend and expand School in the Park–type teaching and learning.

1. Grade-level standards must drive the selection of environments, activities, materials, and assessments.
2. Grade-level standards can be taught and reinforced via hands-on, interdisciplinary, and experiential learning.
3. Formal (directed) and informal (constructive) learning need not be polar opposites.
4. Nontraditional classroom environments, when carefully selected, can provide motivation, purpose, and a depth of understanding for a standards-based curriculum.
5. If nontraditional classroom environments are to be effective in supporting a standards-based curriculum, then the instructional program must coordinate classroom and nonclassroom learning. The curriculum must be mapped and integrated into a year-long subject-specific pacing chart that identifies key standards that will be taught and assessed.
6. The number of nontraditional classroom environments accessible to most schools is limitless and can be inventoried via an environmental scan. Not all of these environments will require extensive logistical arrangements and costs.
7. Extending learning outside of traditional classroom settings creates an opportunity to expand instructors and create teaching teams. Time to engage all of the teaching adults in common planning is time well spent and can serve to support multiple classes and programs.
8. Extending learning outside of traditional classroom settings can increase the prior knowledge students bring to future learning environments and thereby increase their cultural capital.

FIG. 1.1. Replicable key principles for moving beyond field trips.

OFF-CAMPUS LEARNING: FIELD TRIPS AND BEYOND

The field trip is often seen as a reward used for good behavior or for completing a unit of study. In today's world, field trips often conjure up thoughts of unfocused playtime where the confines of the typical classroom give way to relaxed amusement in a casual, unstructured setting. Rather than a significant learning experience, field trips are seen as a time for fun, to relax and take a break from the rigors of learning associated with the traditional classroom and school. Most teachers do not sufficiently plan or align the field trip experience with standards taught in their class. Teachers do, however, spend considerable time getting ready for these one-visit events. The demands on time are often limited to bus requests, permission slips, and lunch arrangements. Often the follow-up activities consist of thank-you letters sent to those who toured the class.

During traditional field trips, students may not learn to appreciate, and behave in, the museums and their exhibits. Teachers spend a great deal of their energy herding the group from exhibit to exhibit. There is often far more crowd control than teaching occurring. Field trip destinations are often big, strange places filled with unfamiliar exhibits and collections to look at, but not touch. The museum guides and educators are also unfamiliar with the class and their curriculum. So the field trip often becomes a day to be away from school, a semi-holiday. At School in the Park, the students become familiar with the museum and feel comfortable with the setting and with the museum educators. They take pride in being students of a prestigious institution. As one student noted at the Museum of Photographic Arts, "This is my museum."

At School in the Park, learning at the museum is taken seriously. When David, a fourth-grade student, saw some field trip students frantically chasing around, he asked his teacher, "Don't they know they are here to learn?" School in the Park students recognize the abundance of material that is available to them. They are constantly saying that they like the program because they learn things they couldn't learn at school and that they know more about certain topics than their siblings.

As schools experience budget cuts, and with increased pressure to improve student performance, field trip budgets are often the first to get cut. Some still argue the value of field trips and lament their demise, but their arguments pale in comparison to those demanding a focus on learning, a focus on standards and on increased testing. Thus, learning outside of the traditional classroom has been devalued and is disappearing from much of public education. It is enough to make John Dewey turn in his grave!

If field trips distract students and teachers from focusing on formal learning, their days will be numbered. This is a time of high-stakes accountability that has quantified the untenable numbers of children who read and compute significantly below grade level. Instructional time is a premium and anything seen as a distraction will not find itself welcome, especially in low-performing inner-city schools.

Its designers are quick to let you know that School in the Park is not a field trip. Why? Field trips have become an educational frill, often described and criticized as being an extra often detracting from critical learning time. There is a need to reconceptualize and reorganize resources associated with traditional field trips to support the type of teaching and learning that occurs in School in the Park. Usually schoolchildren come to the museums on field trips that involve little if any preplanning between the school and museum educator. They visit one or two museums and then return to school. Their role is that of an observer. At School in the Park, the approach is different. The museum is the classroom and the student is a participant in the learning process. The museum educators and the teachers are the guides. The resources of the museums are used to teach and enhance the curriculum.

Like Dewey, many educators know important learning can, and indeed must, occur outside the four walls of traditional classroom settings. Can we think beyond the notion of what field trips have become? Can we reinvest in the use of multiple learning environments as a means of promoting learning? Can a new resurgence of teaching and learning outside the classroom be initiated that contributes to, rather than detracts from, the need to focus on learning, on standards, and on testing? The answer is yes, yes, and yes again! School in the Park offers convincing evidence that community-based learning experiences are relevant to not only improving test scores, but are essential to student motivation and a deeper and richer level of learning and understanding.

WHAT IS SCHOOL IN THE PARK: THE PARTICIPANTS AND THE SETTING

School in the Park creates an immersion program founded in research and based on rigorous curriculum standards developed by the State of California. The program takes place in Balboa Park, a large urban park containing numerous cultural and scientific institutions in the heart of San Diego, California. The architects of the program included a group of school and museum educators and administrators brought together through the vision of a business and social entrepreneur. Sol and Robert Price are well known throughout the retail industry. Many of the warehouse retail stores that permeate the country owe a great debt to the Prices for the innovations they introduced in their Price Club stores. Price Charities' investment in innovative community development initiatives has brought that same entrepreneurial vision and organizational expertise to bear in the public sector throughout San Diego. Their resources, coupled with both their interest in public schools and their involvement with San Diego arts and cultural institutions, led to the School in the Park experiment.

School in the Park began in 1999 as part of the larger City Heights Educational Collaborative. The City Heights Educational Collaborative is a unique partnership between San Diego State University, the San Diego Unified School District, the San Diego Education Association, and Price Charities. A primary goal of the Collaborative is to positively impact the academic achievement of students in three City Heights schools. The schools collectively serve over 5,300 students and include one elementary, one middle, and one high school. Each school has a free and reduced lunch rate of 99% and serves a very culturally, ethnically, and linguistically diverse student body. The goals of the Collaborative are to operate public community schools in which student achievement is accelerated and future, new, and experienced teachers are supported to be effective in inner-city schools.

The community of City Heights faces many challenges. These challenges can be used to paint a very negative picture of City Heights. City Heights has long been considered one of the most dangerous and disadvantaged sections of San Diego—an area plagued by gangs, unemployment, and the lowest school test scores in the district. But, due to the efforts to revitalize City Heights, it now offers a much more positive alternative picture. More than 72,000 people live in a 3,000-acre triangle at the center of the nation's sixth largest city. City Heights is the first stop for many new immigrants from underdeveloped countries, with 40 different cultural groups represented and over 100 dialects spoken. The community is 41% Hispanic, 21% African-American, 20% Asian/Pacific Islander, and 18% White. Forty percent of adults have not completed high school, compared to 18% citywide. In 2001, the median income was $20,000 in a region where the median housing price is now over $350,000. The majority (65%) of City Heights residents live in rental apartments. Thirty-five percent of the residents live at poverty level or below, and unemployment is more than double the citywide average (12.6% vs. 5.9%). City Heights schools have been among the lowest performing in the State of California. Within this context, a large public/private initiative began 10 years ago to revitalize City Heights. New parks, new schools, new stores, new community programs and services are all part of this vigorous and holistic effort. Rosa Parks Elementary is right in the middle of this redevelopment effort and School in the Park is one of the fruits of this labor.

THE SCHOOL IN THE PARK EXPERIENCE: THINKING BEYOND FIELD TRIPS

One day in Balboa Park in downtown San Diego, California, an out-of-town visitor noticed a line of bright-eyed uniformed third graders toting identical backpacks quietly walking through the porticos linking the museums and gardens of the center city park and cultural center. Impressed with their good behavior and their studious air he asked the teacher, "Who are these children? What private school do they attend?" He was informed that these children were students of School in the Park, a program affiliated with Rosa Parks Elementary, a public San Diego school. "What is School in the Park?" he asked. "I've never heard of it."

School in the Park is an extension of Rosa Parks Elementary School serving 1,600 kindergarten through fifth graders within a rich context of culturally and linguistically diverse students. Originally designed as a solution to overcrowding at Rosa Parks Elementary School, the program was embraced by the teachers because of the possibilities they saw to provide their students a world-class education. In this context, all third-, fourth-, and fifth-grade students at Rosa Parks, over 800 students, spend 20% to 25% of their instructional year away from Rosa Parks' main campus in specially selected museums located in San Diego's Balboa Park. The Balboa Park educational experience has been aptly named School in the Park. It represents a significant program that positively impacts how, in this case, children from low-income, inner-city, and culturally diverse backgrounds can experience education in a fundamentally different way.

School in the Park, as the name implies, shifts the location of school from traditional classroom settings, in an inner-city community, to include the outstanding resources and educational opportunities available in the many museums and zoo located in Balboa Park. More than an isolated field trip, School in the Park allows students and teachers to experience expanded learning opportunities for approximately one fourth of their instructional year. Teaching and learning are immersed in the rich resources of world-renowned cultural institutions that are clustered together within a central park setting. School in the Park significantly alters the normal educational setting and methodologies for students and teachers by moving school into the larger community. Unlike the traditional and more episodic nature of field trips, School in the Park is a structured learning experience that focuses on high student expectations aligned with rigorous state education standards. Each day, students spend time learning and gaining new experiences within rich museum settings establishing and building new knowledge influencing their subsequent learning. These learning experiences are cumulative, impacting and influencing both the students' learning in their regular school classroom and in future museum visits. Only time will tell, but all participants and observers seem to agree that the sophistication of prior knowledge these students are gaining and using will not only positively impact their test scores but also their future opportunities, career decisions, and performance.

SCHOOL IN THE PARK: A UNIQUE EXPERIENCE

The concept of blending informal and formal learning opportunities through School in the Park has represented an unparalleled educational alternative. There are a few examples of full-time charter schools located within museums. However, the number of students, teachers, and museums involved in School in the Park coupled with the amount of time students spend there is unique. As an example, New York City Museum School services about 360 sixth- through twelfth-grade students who are taught by classroom teachers in a museum setting. NYCMS students work in five museums for two and one half afternoons a week. A lottery system selects students for this program. School in the Park services 800 third-, fourth-, and fifth-grade students in 10 museums (including the San Diego Zoo) each year. Students can spend 1 out of every 4 or 5 weeks in the museums (over 3 years this adds up to 24 weeks). Every third-, fourth-, and fifth-grade student who attends Rosa Parks Elementary participates.

Many students from more affluent families and communities may more regularly be exposed to a variety of cultural settings and experiences, but offering these types of experiences to students who attend large inner-city public schools is rare. Nieto (2003) argued that inner-city schools are least likely to provide their students creative, energetic, and challenging environments. Critics of the standards-based curriculum reform movement suggest high-stakes testing has increased this problem as schools scramble to remediate students. Not so at School in the Park. Students are offered a *rigorous and relevant* standards-based curriculum.

School in the Park incorporates a continuous improvement process using achievement test data to identify standards and skills that must be more effectively addressed within the program. Some proponents of informal education may shudder at the notion of being so data driven. As a school serving students who are still considered low performing, school leadership cannot afford to not be data driven. However, in its first 5 years of operation, School in the Park's attention to standards appears to compromise nothing that would alarm either the traditional educator or the informal constructivist.

Students and teachers within School in the Park are changing the way they see and experience the world. Moving into the larger community, students are stepping up to new and challenging learning experiences that expose them to a world far broader than the confines of City Heights. As one teacher from Rosa Parks describes the program, "School in the Park is more relevant for my students because they are able to apply what they learn in real settings that just cannot be replicated in my classroom." Dr. Arthur Ollman, Director of the Museum of Photographic Arts, describes the impact of School in the Park, "As a result of their experience, the museum now belongs to these students." Sooner than not, it is hoped that these same students will learn the whole world belongs to them.

School in the Park represents a significant part of the overall efforts of the City Heights Educational Collaborative to improve educational outcomes. Rosa Parks continues to demonstrate academic improvement well beyond the growth targets established by the State of California. The Academic Performance Index (API) is the accountability system created by the State of California. The API is a formula that measures a school's overall test performance and growth. Each year school growth targets are set to close the gap, over time, between low-performing and well-performing schools. The State of California uses API scores to assess both individual school progress and to compare a school's performance with other schools in the state. From 2000–2001 to 2002–2003, Rosa Parks has demonstrated a 181-point growth in the API. For these 3 years Rosa Parks exceeded its API targets by over 100%, making it among the top 25% in the city. In 1999 Rosa Parks ranked 5th among its 10 comparison schools; in 2003 and 2004 it ranked 1st. This remarkable trend continues.

Organization and Structure

The design of the program was assigned to a school administrator with an off-campus, educational background who now serves as the School in the Park Director and who provides daily focus and direction to insure consistent program implementation. The program staff includes a lead teacher who, with the director, assists in curriculum development, teacher and student support, and general program administration. Five part-time aides provide additional assistance during instructional time and lunch.

The challenge in designing this program was to insure that the curriculum standards were formally addressed while the students were at the museums. Museum education is sometimes considered informal education, not tied to a structured curriculum. By having classroom teachers and museum educators work together to create curriculum maps to align grade-level standards with resources and exhibits that were part of the museums' collections, the design of the program allowed a blending of informal/formal education. The collaboration of the museum educators and the Rosa Parks teachers resulted in a focus on content standards while creating an effective and motivating instructional design. The museum provides a wonderful context for learning opportunities and educators can, with sufficient time and support, provide and integrate formal and informal learning (Hooper-Greenhill, 1999).

School in the Park is a dynamically changing program with significant modifications that have occurred during the first 5 years of operation. From serving half of the third grade in school year 1999–2000, the program grew from 125 students to include the entire third and fourth grades in school year 2000–2001 for a total of 540 students. By the beginning of school year 2001–2002 the fifth grade was added to now serve over 800 students working within 10 museums.

During the school year, an average of 200 students attend School in the Park each day. Typically, students arrive in the park at 8:40 a.m. after a 20-minute bus ride. Importantly, the bus ride is used as instructional time. Teachers organize materials needed to facilitate individualized and group activities on the bus. While at the museums, museum educators lead the first 2 hours of instruction (9 a.m.–11 a.m.). During this time the Rosa Parks teacher remains with the class and provides support for the museum educator. This is especially helpful for students who are learning English as a second language in that the teacher can provide for interpretation and clarification as needed. The museum educators use museum exhibit areas and classroom space for instruction. After the 2-hour museum lesson, the Rosa Parks teacher directs lessons for the rest of the instructional day. There is a half-hour lunch break during which students are served bag lunches in one of the outdoor areas of the park. After lunch, teachers choose either to further expand on the day's museum lesson or to address other instructional needs. Students depart for the return trip home to Rosa Parks at 1:40 p.m.

Museum educators serve as liaisons for the museums and work closely with the Rosa Parks teachers. The classroom teachers stay with their students and team with the museum educators. The School in the Park program operates on a revolving schedule where students typically spend 1 week in a museum followed by 3 or 4 weeks back at Rosa Parks Elementary School. Each museum is assigned as a third-, fourth-, or fifth-grade museum and is revisited one to three times during the school year. Hence students experience 7 to 9 weeks of School in the Park per year and learn in three or four museums each year. Museums are assigned to a grade level on the basis of how well the exhibits align with state standards for that grade level. As students progress through the program in each grade, they experience different museums. The program design includes a lead museum educator who is associated with each of the participating museums and the San Diego Zoo.

Teacher Expectations. It is interesting to note that although the curriculum is rigorous, teachers believe the students are capable of more and so the level of instruction continually increases. This is one of the very beneficial elements of School in the Park. When teachers see their students excelling at what might be considered "difficult" concepts for inner-city students, their expectations for their students reach a new level. The 1st year some teachers complained that studies were too hard. By the end of that year, teachers extolled the capabilities of their students—they could do anything. Classroom teachers have been enthusiastic about the changes in their student expectations. They are reevaluating their old lessons to fit these needs. Some of the lessons they used in the past no longer meet their new levels of expectation. Teachers comment that they are constantly increasing the level of difficulty and sophistication of their lessons. Seeing children respond positively to these new levels has been exciting for the teachers.

Professional Development. Professional development is an ongoing practice. Because of its unique nature, School in the Park is breaking new ground and constantly evaluating its results. Museum educators and

Rosa Parks teachers meet three times annually to discuss and evaluate the program. Museum curriculum is distributed a few weeks before a teacher brings his or her class to the park and this allows teachers to prepare their students for the visit. Curriculum includes background information for the teacher, descriptions of what will be covered during the museum teacher's time, vocabulary to be used during the week, possible activities to use before the museum visit, bus work ideas, and follow-up suggestions.

Electronic mail plays an important role in keeping communication lines open between the Rosa Parks teachers and the museum educators. Teachers talk back and forth with their colleagues about new exhibits, classroom activities, and other related subjects that might support the School in the Park experience. Museums are happy to give teacher passes to the Rosa Parks staff for independent teacher studies at the museums.

Parent Involvement. Parents are also encouraged to participate in School in the Park. They are welcome to ride the bus with their child and spend the day or week with them. A few parents do spend the entire time with their child. However, many come just for a day or to observe a particular activity. The museums have also encouraged parent participation by distributing tickets for special events at the museums for parents and other family members. Focus groups of parents monitoring overall parent satisfaction with the program are ongoing.

Impact of School in the Park on Museums

The impact of School in the Park on museums has been very positive. In meetings with museum personnel, several benefits have been highlighted. Although collaborations among the museums have always been good, School in the Park has made them stronger. Working on the same project has allowed museum staffs to benefit from the curriculum of other museums and to learn new strategies and techniques for teaching. The curriculum that is used for School in the Park is also now used by other school groups and visitors. Museum personnel report that School in the Park has raised the level of education in Balboa Park. More staff in the education departments has allowed continued support of the educational programs in many museums. Several museums have replicated some of the School in the Park program with other schools, which has been financially beneficial to the museums as well as creating a larger attendance of students in the museums. The program has also helped fulfill the mission of education for many of the museums. Although the mission statement has always been education, some museum staffs now look at education in a new light. They have a whole new view of what education is and can be. And while enhancing credibility with funders and accreditation committees, museums have stated that School in the Park has been helpful in obtaining new grants for their institutions.

One challenge that has been stated by the museums for expanding the program is classroom space. Most museums do not have the space needed to increase the number of schools participating in the program. When schools do come, they are scheduled around School in the Park. The other challenge for the museums is creating assessment tools that help determine student progress. This, however, is an overall challenge of the program because there are so many areas to assess.

ABOUT THE ORGANIZATION OF THIS BOOK: SUBJECT SPECIFIC OR INTERDISCIPLINARY?

When we try to pick out anything by itself, we find it hitched to everything else in the universe.

—John Muir

Proponents of School in the Park argue that the program is a part of a consistent, rigorous, standards-based curriculum. Additionally proponents argue that the program is hands-on and interdisciplinary and uses best instructional practices. The very organization of this book is designed to objectively verify these assertions. Authors were chosen because each had a subject area and instructional expertise. Each was asked to critique School in the Park on the basis of that expertise. As a result the bulk of the chapters analyze School in the Park based on its adherence to subject-specific standards and subject-specific pedagogy. Thus the editors made a decision that the book would be organized by subject matter. However, when considering the chapters as a whole instead of as isolated units, an interesting phenomenon occurs. Namely, the program proved itself to be quite interdisciplinary. It so happened that several authors unknowingly chose to analyze the same museums and activities. The editors' first reaction was to go back to the authors and ask them to choose different activities for analysis and exemplification. That is, our first reaction was to eliminate the "redundancy." Rethinking this reaction occurred as we considered the value of "instructional redundancy" (e.g., Clark & Mayer, 2003). Redundancy for a purpose, and the purpose was to exemplify interdisciplinary programming at its best. Each author or group of authors analyzed the activity based on their subject matter assignment and the same activity passed the test of multiple authors focusing on different subjects!

For example, the gold rush is analyzed in chapters 3, 6, and 8, whereas the Silk Road is considered in chapters 3, 5, 7, and 8, and the Kumeyaay Indians are the focus of chapters 3, 4, and 6. We encourage the reader to consider the power of a single activity addressing multiple standards in multiple subject areas. We argue that the approach makes and encourages connections and offers students a whole new way of making sense of the world.

The hands-on and interdisciplinary nature of the instruction helps children make connections from one subject to another. Children are becoming more critical thinkers and are able to integrate their academic knowledge with their experience. For example, fourth-grade students study the human skeletal system as part of their science curriculum. At the Museum of Man, the students studied ancient Egypt. Math and science standards were integrated into their Egyptian study. Students learned details of measurement and the human skeletal system by examining and measuring mummy bones. This, in turn, triggered a great interest in Egypt. Books were flying off the shelf at the Rosa Parks Elementary School library. Students wanted more and more information about mummies, pharaohs, pyramids, and anything Egyptian, hence literary standards were also addressed. Other connections are noted among the students. When visiting the IMAX theatre, the students were told to be very quiet because a whisper could be heard from one end of the theatre to the other. On hearing this, Ulysses, an 8-year-old student, commented, "That's because the ceiling is a parabola." Ulysses had learned about parabolas from a lesson on sound at the Reuben H. Fleet Science Center. Another student, when asked if he had found any insects on a walk in the zoo answered, "No, but I found an exoskeleton." The correct use of the word "exoskeleton" for a third-grade student represented an expanding vocabulary and a learning activity in which a word could be used appropriately. In class one day, visiting dignitaries were pleased to hear a student give an impromptu oral presentation explaining how static electricity works. The information came from an earlier experience at the Reuben H. Fleet Science Center.

These connections and perspectives also foster what Sizer (1997) called habits of mind; that is, new ways of organizing oneself as a learner and of conceptualizing environments and events. The educational museum visits foster the ability of students to use, manage, and complete tasks/assignments as they wander through the museum. The museum environments also provided to be quite interactive. Authors noted how this "learn by doing" opportunity also fostered these habits of mind. In his discussion concerning learning in interactive environments, Roschelle (1995) suggested that the use of interactivity could afford an opportunity for different students with different prior knowledge and varied talents to access information and to learn by interacting with the same exhibit.

For example, most children are familiar with airplanes. Most children have some interest in airplanes and would like to travel in one. During their extended time at the Aerospace Museum the students have a chance to study air travel in depth. They look at real planes from the beginning of aviation up to life-size models of spacecraft. They learn about balloons, biplanes, and other forms of flight. They discuss aerodynamics. As part of their learning activity, the students have the opportunity to design their own glider. They are given a problem. How can they make the glider fly better and longer? They experiment with different methods. They work together in groups and exchange ideas and then test out their conclusions. In this activity they learn about and utilize the scientific method. Their knowledge of their world is reinforced and they have the joy of discovery and a sense of achievement.

This joy of discovery and sense of achievement was demonstrated by a fifth-grade student who went home and set up his own experiment based on his knowledge of the scientific method. He wanted to test the principle of Newton's third law of motion, action/reaction. His goal was to find out if a balloon filled with air and released under water would react the same way it did in air. He reported that he had his hypothesis and carried out the experiment. When asked what happened, he said the balloon didn't move at the same rate of speed but that he wondered if he added more water, would he have a different outcome.

Museums can provide relevance by allowing students to become "experts" in various fields as they make connections. For example, at the San Diego Historical Society Museum one way students learn about San Diego history is by going to the archives and looking at old newspapers and pictures. A secondary gain from this activity is acquiring information about the care and preservation of historical materials. The students must wear white gloves, modeling the professional archivists, while handling old materials, and they begin to understand some of the problems involved in working with fragile items from the past. Another student brought her family to the Museum of Art during the spring break to explain to them what it is like to paint on canvas rather than paper.

The interdisciplinary nature of the activities feel more natural and less rigid than, for example, math class. A playful atmosphere may augment a relaxed environment by encouraging hands-on experimentation. Technology-based exhibits are particularly suitable for this. Students are able to personalize the learning environment. They should feel that they can wander and explore at will (Semper, 1990). Also contributing to a relaxed atmosphere is the fact that museum visits occur within a social context. The interdisciplinary nature of the activity and the interactive environment facilitates joint experimentation (Semper, 1990). Conversations that involve debate, clarification, and discussion of exhibits may lead to more profound learning.

Interdisciplinary interactive learning facilitates real-life connections, making lessons appear less abstract and more relevant. When properly integrated, students discover the practicality and immediacy of academic subjects. For example, in the Hall of Champions, in a study called Fantasy Baseball, students are taught fractions, decimals, percentages, and ratios with baseball cards and score cards. Youngsters study and manipulate the statistics using mathematical operations to create a baseball team. The teams then play against each other in tournament style. Students see the relevance of math, not only as an academic topic, but how math works in real life. They are able to see how knowledge fits into a broader world. Their expectations are expanded and the future looks exciting and promising. The work is challenging. Students respond to challenge.

REFERENCES

Clark, R. C., & Mayer, R. E. (2003). Does practice make perfect? In *e-learning and the science of instruction* (pp. 149–171). San Francisco: Pfeiffer.

Hooper-Greenhill, E. (1999). *The educational role of the museum.* London: Routledge.

Nieto, S. (2003). *Affirming diversity: The sociopolitical context of multicultural education* (4th ed.). Boston: Allyn & Bacon.

Roschelle, J. (1995). *Learning in interactive environments: Prior knowledge and new experience.* Retrieved March 28, 2003, from http://www.astc.org/resource/educator/priorknw.htm

Semper, R. J. (1990). *Science museums as environments for learning.* Retrieved April 1, 2003, from http://www.astc.org.resource/educator/scimus.htm

Sizer, T. R. (1997). *Horace's hope: What works for the American high school.* New York: Mariner Books.

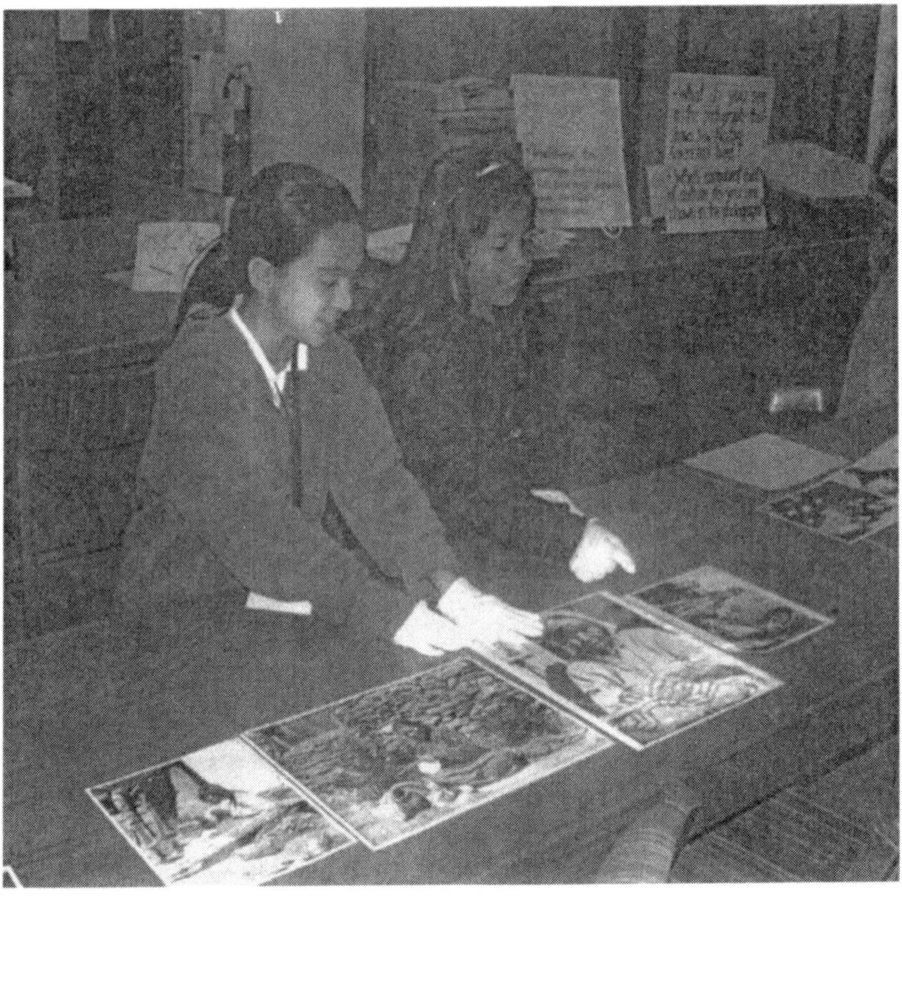

CHAPTER TWO

Perspectives on Learning—Creating Optimal Conditions for Learning

Ian Pumpian
Maria Grant
Susan Wachowiak

School in the Park operationalizes learning strategies that are well represented in learning theory literature, including multiple intelligences (Armstrong, 2003; Gardner, 1983/1993), constructivism (Brooks & Brooks, 1999), differentiated instruction (Tomlinson, 2003), authentic assessment (Marzano, Pickering, & McTighe, 2000), and project- and problem-based learning (Torp & Sage, 2002). It is beyond the scope of this book to trace the components of School in the Park to each of these theoretical constructs, although proponents of each should have no problem making the connections. Instead in this chapter we ground School in the Park by employing four related constructs. First, we grounded our chapter 1 discussion of School in the Park as an extension of interdisciplinary instruction (Jacobs, 1997), as we feel the program encourages students to make connections and allows students to access content via their individual skills and interests. Throughout the book readers will notice different subject area critiques reference the same instructional activities. Thus the same instructional unit covered multiple content area standards.

Second, we chose to reference Csikszentmihalyi's works on "flow" as so much of the work of School in the Park assumes internal motivation and learning processes. Third, we chose to use the terminology of "informal" learning and "formal" learning and the constructs each implies because these terms are common in museums and museum educational programs and also because we advocate throughout this book that programs can in fact blend the two without compromising the basic tenets of either. The benefits of curriculum mapping and using literacy-rich environments are reviewed.

Finally, we chose to reference "cultural capital" as a construct, as we argue that School in the Park may fill a void in the prior knowledge poor students bring to the learning environment and in so doing increase the cultural capital they need in order to be successful students. Throughout this chapter, we offer examples of literacy-rich environments where additional personnel, materials, and resources add to each student's cultural capital.

FLOW: OPTIMIZING LEARNING AND PERFORMANCE

Most sports enthusiasts are familiar with the phrase "in the zone." The reference is commonly applied when some superstar's play raises to a level well beyond the rest of the field. The player is described as being locked in, while the performance appears effortless and over the top. When such a performance is observed, a positive outcome seems certain. Scientifically this "in the zone" experience has received considerable attention as a result of the work of Mihaly Csikszentmihalyi and his colleagues (e.g., 1975, 1988, 1999). More specifically, they have studied a phenomenon they have labeled as " flow." In the past 10 years the study of flow has expanded from one of more general motivation, creativity, and performance to include possible school and educational implications and usages.

Imagine creating learning situations in which more students and classes of students generally and frequently could be considered "in the zone," learning situations in which motivation, skill, and engagement lead to more of the same. Furthermore imagine a learning situation in which the curricular content is fully aligned with state and federal standards and frameworks, the very standards and frameworks that proponents contend are necessary to attend to if student achievement is to measurably improve but critics argue lead to the dullest and least creative forms of teaching and learning. In this chapter we suggest that School in the Park creates conditions that are conducive with flow as suggested by Csikszentmihalyi's research. As is described, the key seems to be the planned and purposeful blending of formal learning and informal learning opportunities in environments that are both content and literacy rich, as well as likely to elicit the interests and talents of a very diverse group of students. The museums of Balboa Park provide such a setting and the curriculum mapping that public school and museum educators are engaged in provide for that unique blend. Curriculum mapping has provided the organizational structure necessary to assure that blend of learning occurs at School in the Park. The use of the museums as classrooms and the curriculum mapping that guides the teaching and learning activities that occur there will be further described and exemplified in this chapter.

Most educators today realize the potential for learning within the context of a museum setting. This is manifest by the sheer numbers of museum excursions arranged by teachers and other youth leaders across the country on an annual basis. It is estimated that over 250,000 children visit Balboa Park museums annually. What seems to elude those in charge of leading students through such educational encounters is the means by which to truly capture and focus the attention of the students in a way that evokes creative and critical thinking on the part of the learners. Also missed is the opportunity to use the excursion as a time for students with varying abilities and backgrounds to discover knowledge in different ways. Despite this, the possibility for profound educational experiences exists. The mode by which to tap into the rich offerings, presented by curators and exhibit directors, needs to be explored.

Visitors to museums often express the desire to combine learning with enjoyment (Falk & Dierking, 2000). Given the opportunity for built-in motivation, it is natural for schools to offer field excursions to zoos, aquariums, and art galleries. If the goal is to use such visits to augment and expand classroom learning, then the curriculum development must construct meaning as a student wanders through an exhibit. It is with this thought in mind that School in the Park advanced the effort to incorporate the learning opportunities found in Balboa Park into the daily curriculum. Intrinsic enjoyment of learning seems to be connected to higher creativity (Csikszentmihalyi & Hermanson, 1995). Museum exhibits offer the possibility of profound learning and creative expression. Thus, the exploration of ways in which such an experience may be promoted is of foremost significance. Meeting the needs of a diverse student population, fostering a desire to learn, and a feeling of joy and involvement with learning (i.e., flow) are driving forces behind School in the Park.

Teachers, parents, and youth group leaders typically plan excursions to museums because they want to have fun while acquiring new knowledge (Semper, 1990). Visitors tend to wander and may only choose to view some exhibits and not others. Some children who are not considered successful learners in traditional classrooms have proven themselves to be profound learners in the context of a museum setting (Gardner, 1983/1993). Museum exhibits are accessible to students with a wide range of interests and abilities. When students explore concepts in a museum setting, they may be more likely to understand the concept when it is again presented in the traditional classroom. In the same manner that the wood of a guitar vibrates in sympathy with the pluck of a string, a student will experience "resonance" when curricular material is first encountered in another setting and then reintroduced in the school classroom (Garnder, 1983/1993).

Blending Formal and Informal Learning

Combining rigorous academic standards with authentic learning is what makes School in the Park so unique. Students who attend School in the Park experience both academic (formal) and authentic (informal) learning. In formal learning, which is typically and commonly associated with K through 12 education, students are required to learn certain materials and acquire specific skills (i.e., reading, writing, and arithmetic). Instruction tends to be more teacher directed. Proponents believe that formal learning is strongly tied to the concept that students need to acquire a good foundation of knowledge that will be needed as they progress through their educational career. However, the benefits of this foundation may not be apparent to the students. Some students may question why they need to learn certain skills and are told that they will need it later in their schooling.

Museums have purported to be settings in which learning is often more "informal" (Hein, 1998). Informal learning emphasizes a process of self-discovery and intrinsic motivation. Learning tends to be less directed by others and the learner is much more involved in determining the parameters, value, purpose, and goals of an experience. "Hands-on" and "minds-on" activities can more directly involve the student in the educational process and allow them to become more motivated learners. With their content knowledge and authentic experiences, students use their skills and see the results of their learning. Advocates believe that with increased motivation students enjoy learning and will become lifelong learners.

School in the Park demonstrates that formal and informal education can be successfully blended by combining academic standards and authentic learning. The results are dramatic. Students who were historically among the lowest achieving students in the state are now changing a profile of failure into one of success. School in the Park promotes both academic excellence and increased motivation for students by recognizing student strengths and building on those strengths. We believe School in the Park is an important and innovative method that positively impacts educational outcomes. Through a deeper understanding of the key features of this program, we hope to influence other communities to implement similar projects.

Curriculum Mapping. The museum provides a wonderful context for learning opportunities and educators can, with sufficient time and support, provide and integrate formal and informal learning (Hooper-Greenhill, 1999). However, the process begins well before an excursion is planned. The success of School in the Park begins with a focus on standards. A school must align its curriculum to key standards. Key standards clearly delineate content that will be taught in each grade level as well as how each grade level scaffolds the learning that will take place the following year. Jacobs (1997) referred to this as horizontal and vertical curriculum alignment. Teachers then map out their year in order to make sure time will be devoted to each key standard and in a logical flow. Assessments are designed and selected that provide feedback regarding student learning and proficiency on the key standards. Teachers then select, plan, and secure the materials, lessons, and experiences deemed most effective in teaching the key standards and associated skills. In this process, Rosa Parks teachers have considered when and where nontraditional classrooms (aka the museums) can be an effective part of this design. Thus museum-based instruction is not an afterthought or treated as a break from or additive to the curriculum. As years go by, the use of the museum, the activities that are planned, and the logistical arrangements that need to be made become integrated into the teachers' curriculum maps and instructional program. Museum educators can, in turn, employ these standards-based activities with other groups who come to visit—and learn—in the museums.

School in the Park utilizes the resources of the museums to fulfill the basics of the school curriculum and California state standards in mathematics, science, language arts, social studies, and the visual and performing arts. The challenge in designing this program was to insure that the curriculum standards were addressed while the students were at the museums. At first this was a major challenge because museum education is usually considered to be informal education and not tied to a structured curriculum. The problem was solved by having classroom teachers and museum educators work together to create curriculum maps to align grade-level standards with resources and exhibits that were part of the museums' collections. The collaboration of the instructors and the teachers resulted in focus on content standards while creating an effective and motivating instructional design. The museum and school administrators also were critical to this process by working to coordinate the specific museums that would be visited by which grades, and when in the year those visits would happen.

The curriculum maps are detailed calendars of the content, skills, and assessment that the curriculum requires for each grade level at a particular time. For example, for September and October, one of the content standards in mathematics for third grade requires the student analyzes plane and solid geometric objects and their attributes. Included in the skills to be learned are: (a) identify, name, describe, and classify polygons; (b) use correct vocabulary for polygon attributes: line segment AB, vertex, vertices, faces, edges, and so on; (c) name and describe common dimensional geometric objects; (d) identify, draw, and describe attributes of polygons,

(e) understand length versus width; (f) understand area versus perimeter; and (g) compute areas in square inches and square centimeters. The assessment tools are: (a) activities from Quest 2000 Unit 7, (b) *Math By All Means—Geometry*, and (c) unit tests.

The curriculum maps provide this information for each grade and each subject: mathematics, science, language arts, and social studies. The maps give the month or months that the content should be taught with mastery of the total content the goal for the year. The museum educators and the classroom teachers meet at the beginning of each year and use these maps to coordinate their efforts. The museum educators examine their museum exhibits and collections to see how they could be utilized to teach the content. For example, at the Museum of Art, the museum educators realized that the exhibit on modern art could be used to teach geometric shapes. By working together, museum teachers and classroom teachers were able to write interdisciplinary curriculum that addressed multiple content areas. This is beneficial to the classroom teachers as they are accountable for the students achieving the content standard goals. It is also beneficial for the museum educators because they learned about the curriculum and they are also able to use this information to make the lessons given to "field trip" students from other schools more relevant to the standards.

Many times students from the inner city have not had many "out of the neighborhood" experiences. Consequently, they do not always have the background information or prior knowledge to connect new information. By attending classes at the museums, students are inundated with visual, auditory, and kinesthetic information. Displays and exhibits at the institutions offer a feast of information for students to explore. These exhibits also present the appropriate vocabulary for the subject. While studying at the Museum of Natural History, fourth-grade students are taught geological principles. They study the rock cycle, land formations, and plate tectonics. They acquire a foundation of information concerning this subject. As students advance in their academic careers and are presented with more information on geology, they will be able to build on this foundation. Students acquire a context in which to place the new material. A focus on academic excellence provides School in the Park students with the knowledge they need to achieve their current and future academic goals.

Literacy-Rich Environments. One of the most credible components for blending informal and formal learning in School in the Park is the fact that the museum environments are arguably the literacy-rich environments most teachers try to emulate in their traditional classrooms. The literacy-rich museums coupled with interactivity, hands-on offerings, and/or the display of authentic articles can inspire awe, fear, a sense of thrill, and even pique curiosity (Carlson, 1998). What child would not be both thrilled and fearful at the sight of shrunken heads as is seen in the Museum of Man in San Diego's Balboa Park? Or consider the way in which curiosity can be piqued at the Museum of Art when students study the Renaissance by becoming apprentices at the Great Firenza Studio. They are introduced to the architecture, clothing, geography, customs, and artists of the time and period by slides, pictures, and books, and they design apprentice hats to wear at the museum and in their studio. They go to the European art gallery in the museum to observe how the Renaissance masters depicted life in Renaissance Europe. The curator of European art discusses the paintings with the students. When they go back to the studio they become familiar with the life story of Giuseppi Grazzi, a fictional character of the time who commissions the painting of a panel depicting his life. Students are divided into five teams. With the help of a brief biography of his life, each team paints their interpretation of a period of his life. When the pictures are completed they receive a surprise visit from Giuseppi (a costumed museum educator). He evaluates the paintings and each apprentice receives a gold-wrapped chocolate coin in payment for services rendered. Through these life-based activities students used all the major styles of learning and the Renaissance became an experience rather than just a part of the past.

The literacy-rich environments pique curiosity and interest to attend and because attention is a scare resource, what an individual chooses to attend to is significant (Csikszentmihalyi, 1990). Consider the student experiences at the San Diego Zoo. The students go behind the scenes to see how the zoo specialists work with the animals. The students are taken to "the bedroom area" of the animals and watch how the animals are fed and cared for. Each specialist is an expert in their particular species and many of them have worked with these animals for a long period of time. They know both the behavior and the different personalities of these animals and they are able to share this information with the students who study behavioral adaptation at the zoo. The students are able to develop and experience different perspectives about the animals. Rather than simply walking past animals and cages they get a richer sense that these are living creatures with personalities and histories. Students also have a chance to interact on a personal level with some of the animals. With a baboon named Loon, the students are asked to bring things from home that Loon can safely play with and then students observe his reaction. The students are also allowed to feed some of the animals, such as giraffes, camels, and Galapagos tortoises. While studying the digestive systems of owls, the students discover that owls regurgitate owl pellets. These are small balls of indigestible materials, like bones and hair. The students dissect the pellets and examine the contents. They usually find tiny rodent bones and insect skeletal remains. They compare these remains to a chart that helps them identify the prey and the different types of bones, such as the clavicle, femur, and pelvic bones. Direct participation by the students provides a new appreciation of nature and the environment.

The museums' exhibits, archives, and personnel provide literacy-rich resources a regular classroom cannot typically provide. Using these community resources gives students an opportunity to learn from experts in their field. The museum educators are a conduit to those resources. They have a store of knowledge, a focus, and an enthusiasm for the subject that they teach. They keep up with the latest research. They are familiar with practical applications of their information. They have access to a vast set of materials.

School in the Park allows students to contribute to the literacy-rich settings, not just to observe it. At the Museum of Photographic Arts fourth-grade students produced their interpretation of the Greek tragedy, Orpheus and Eurydice. They started by learning the story and then delving into the emotions and psychological aspects of the play. They were taught how internal feelings could be expressed in the external world through facial expression, body movements, colors, shapes, and sounds. After the play was performed the students wrote about it in the school paper *The City Heights Pilot Post*. The following are excepts from the students' article.

> *The Actors:* "Each of us got a part in the play, but there were no lines for any of the characters. Instead we had to use body movement, demonstration, miming, hand signs like pointing, face expressions, and moving faster or slower to show how the characters felt and who they were. With teamwork and lots of practice we were able to show when our characters were happy, angry, excited, worried, sad, or nervous, and if they were scary, powerful, or friendly. . . . The hardest part was that we had to do it in front of everyone with only one dress rehearsal. . . . It was a little embarrassing . . . but it was also exciting with a real audience. We had the opportunity to perform on stage and not many people get to do that."
>
> *The Photographers:* "Our part in the play was to take pictures of the different settings of the play. . . . We searched through Balboa Park to find good photos. . . . We symbolized Orpheus and Eurydice falling in love and getting married with a photo of bright and colorful flowers. We found a big iron gate at one of the museum buildings for the gates to the underworld, and water in a shadow for the river Styx. The digital cameras we used were cool. We liked taking photos and they helped the play look real."
>
> *The Music and Sound Crew:* "To choose music and sound for the play we thought about the settings and divided the play into 11 parts. We then used an electronic keyboard . . . to make a sound track that would help show what was happening and the feelings or emotions of the actors and scene. We used low and soft or high and loud sounds, or complete quiet to show

anger, sadness, love or happiness, or people or places that were scary, creepy, or nice. . . . We had to work together as a team, and it was hard work but also fun."

This activity at the Museum of Photographic Arts is literacy rich and it fulfills many content standards in language arts. For example, the students are making connections between the play, personal experiences, and prior knowledge. They are also taught to analyze literary elements of a play (e.g., climax, problem solution, protagonist–antagonist) and to describe the setting and analyze characters. By actively participating in the production of the play and reading their reviews, external motivation is increased and they are more likely to want to perform another play.

Dewey would assert that choices about the future and one's direction in life can result from this type of experience. At the Museum of Photographic Arts, through the Greek mythological story of the Minotaur and the maze in which he lived, the students become aware of the analogy of the maze, and are asked to relate it to their life's journey and the many decisions and choices they need to make. "Which Way Will I Turn?" is the topic of a poem each student writes that highlights the student's thoughts on how he or she will chose his or her own particular path. A fourth-grade student wrote this poem.

Which Way Will I Turn?
Will I be bad or good?
Will I go to school or not?
Will I make friends or not?
Will I love or not?
Which way will I go?
Will I turn away or will I keep looking?
Will I go with my Mom or Dad?
Are these difficult choices?
Will I help or turn away?
Will I rob like my brother and not be good?
Or will I be a bank teller?
Which way will I turn?

By creating standards-based instruction in these literacy-rich settings, each learner is actively involved in manipulating the learning activity in order to construct knowledge for himself or herself. Museum field excursions typically offer an array of ways to view a particular topic. For example, the Reuben H. Fleet Science Center in San Diego's Balboa Park presents several exhibits dealing with the study of optics. Information regarding lenses, optical illusions, and wave motion is conveyed using hands-on displays that pique curiosity and require individuals to engage in the thought actions of speculation, contemplation, and examination. It is these actions that often ignite the personal desire to know why—that trigger the need to stretch beyond that that is easily within one's grasp.

If we intend to foster creative thought, then we must provide experiences where rote memorization is not the sole focus of the classroom. A skillful blend of teacher-imposed structure and student autonomy is a natural occurrence in a well-planned museum trip.

The literacy-rich museum settings can provide relevance by allowing students to become "experts" in various fields. For example, at the San Diego Historical Society Museum one way students learn about San Diego history is by going to the archives and looking at old newspapers and pictures. A secondary gain from this activity is acquiring information about the care and preservation of historical materials. The students must wear white gloves, modeling the professional archivists, while handling old materials, and they begin to understand some of the problems involved in working with fragile items from the past. Another student brought her family to the Museum of Art during the spring break and tried to explain to them what it is like to paint on canvas rather than paper.

The informal literacy-rich settings can make the standards-based curriculum accessible for more students. Rigid expectations of a student, either the student's own or those of someone else, may hinder concentration. A playful atmosphere may augment a relaxed environment by encouraging hands-on experimentation. Technology-based exhibits are particularly suitable for this. Visitors must be able to personalize their own space. This means that individuals should feel that they can wander and explore at will (Semper, 1990). Also contributing to a relaxed atmosphere, is the fact that museum visits occur within a social context. This facilitates joint experimentation (Semper, 1990). Conversations that involve debate, clarification, and discussion of exhibits may lead to more profound learning.

Learning outside of the classroom can make lessons appear less abstract and more relevant. When properly integrated, students discover the practicality and immediacy of academic subjects. For example, in the Hall of Champions, in a study called Fantasy Baseball, students are taught fractions, decimals, percentages, and ratios with baseball cards and score cards. Youngsters study and manipulate the statistics using mathematical operations to create a baseball team. The teams then play against each other in tournament style. Students see the relevance of math, not only as an academic topic, but how it works in real life. They are able to see how knowledge fits into a broader world. Their expectations are expanded and the future looks exciting and promising. The work is challenging. Students respond to challenge.

Flow is an experience that generates enjoyment. Enjoyment is a forward movement defined by a sense of novelty and accomplishment. According to Hektner and Csikszentmihalyi (1996), flow experienced in an educational setting promotes intrinsic motivation toward schoolwork. School in the Park educators strive to create a balance between formal and informal learning such that the external expectations and motivation of the school become internalized and extended by the young learner. Do students in School in the Park get lost in the moment? Do exhibits and interactions command their undivided attention? Do the activities lead to students feeling in control as they flow from one moment to the next? We encourage you to consider these questions as you read this text. Perhaps the ideas will just "flow"!

Cultural Capital

The achievement gap that exists between inner-city schools and their more affluent neighbors continues to be the subject of debate, policy, and interventions (e.g., Strickland & Alvermann, 2004). The designers of School in the Park believe we can challenge the extent of that gap. It is curious to note that most of the extended field trips other schools make to Balboa Park are the result of initiatives based in affluent private schools. Nieto (2003) suggested that whereas "failing" schools resort back to regimented remedial chalk-and-talk programs (which she labeled as the pedagogy of poverty), students in schools not pressured by their accountability results sponsor more exciting and engaging hands-on learning. Is this because they do not have to be as concerned with results, or is it perhaps one of the very keys to their success? Does a rich and engaging curriculum lead to better student achievement than a drill-based remedial back-to-basics approach?

One perspective is to consider that student success and achievement has been directly related to the amount of prior and background knowledge each student brings to a learning situation (Marzano, 2004). The type of prior knowledge that affluent students bring to the classroom tends to be more associated with school success than the prior knowledge possessed by students whose families have experienced generational poverty (Payne, 2001). Researchers have proposed these differences in prior knowledge as differences in the cultural capital students possess. In this sense cultural capital would refer to how prepared a student is to enter the learning environment and be successful. Programs such as School in the Park are an investment in each student's capital. We argue that they will enter middle school richer, that is, with prior knowledge that is more conducive to their school success.

In her anthropological study of programs at Rosa Parks, Grove (in press) specifically addressed School in the Park from the perspective of building "cultural capital," a term studied and coined by Bourdieu and

Passeron (1977). Analogous to economic capital, Bourdieu and Passeron argued that cultural capital allows one to maintain, or gain, status. The premise suggests that acquisition of new knowledge and skill is largely a function of socialization and prior knowledge. Bourdieu's research examined the links between class and educational attainment and he concluded that familial exposure to "high-brow culture" is directly related to academic success and is a predictor of it. Grove argued that it is possible to provide this exposure through schools if familiarity with art, classics, and literature is accomplished. Grove concluded that School in the Park can do just that. Extended periods of time and instruction in these museums can result in challenging the limits of social class and can provide students a durable set of beliefs and knowledge that can shape future learning, planning, and performance. As such, School in the Park is a cultural capital investment! Every good teacher knows how to assess, and build off of the prior knowledge each student brings to their classroom. The more prior knowledge a student brings into the classroom the more successful a student they are. As Grove stated: "Beyond knowing the name of a painting or piece of art, such a person can discuss it, analyze it, and form a personal opinion about it. They are comfortable and confident about their abilities, have a natural ease in the cultural world" (in press).

CONCLUSIONS

If museums house the articles, the documents, the works of art that have the potential to stimulate intrinsic motivation, should we not all board the school bus and head off to our local Museum of Natural History? The implications for learners are immense. By extending school beyond the traditional classroom, School in the Park strives to promote "deep understanding." Deep understanding focuses on meaningful patterns using information that is connected (Grotzer, 1996). In contrast to superficial learning that is easily forgotten by the learner, "deep understanding" is usually remembered and may be applied to novel situations. Many teachers today complain that students don't seem to recall recently taught lessons. To combat this, teachers need to focus on extrapolation and connection making (Grotzer, 1996). Museum, aquarium, and zoo exhibits provide real-world objects that can promote these conditions. So too might a local estuary, a food store, or a factory. When deep understanding does occur, students can be guided by instructors toward the transfer of knowledge to new situations. Learning should not be fleeting; it needs to withstand time.

School in the Park has given this opportunity to numerous young people. Educators across the globe have the power to offer such learning experiences to children in their own communities. It is clear that these learning opportunities should extend beyond the typical "once-a-year" field trip. Nonclassroom environments need to be well integrated into the curricular maps teachers construct. Repeated visits to museums allow for extensive probing and the development of "deep understanding." These visits might as well be collaborations with scientists and others. Collaborations between museum educators, classroom teachers, and other adults must be established. In addition, instruction based on the research needs to be put in place. Ultimately it is the school leaders who must take the reins to move forward beyond the campus parking lot in search of novel environments, motivation, inspiration, and connections to life. The following chapters discuss the nitty-gritty behind the subject-specific integration of standards-based curriculum into a museum, aquarium, or zoo setting.

REFERENCES

Armstrong, T. (2003). *The multiple intelligences of reading and writing: Making the words come alive*. Alexandria, VA: Association of Supervision and Curriculum Development.

Bourdieu, P., & Passeron, J. C. (1977). *Reproduction in education, society and culture* (R. Nice, Trans.). Beverly Hills, CA: Sage.

Brooks, J. G., & Brooks, M. G. (1999). *In search of understanding: The case for constructivist classrooms* (Rev. ed.). Alexandria, VA: Association of Supervision and Curriculum Development.

Carlson, S. (1998). *Learning by doing and the youth-driven model*. Retrieved April 3, 2003, from http://www.fourh.umn.edu/educators/research/center/PDF/Center-Story8.pdf

Csikszentmihalyi, M. (1975). *Beyond boredom and anxiety*. San Francisco: Jossey-Bass.

Csikszentmihalyi, M. (1990). *Flow: The psychology of optimal experience*. New York: Harper & Row.

Csikszentmihalyi, M. (1999). *Flow: The psychology of optimal experience* (Reproduction ed.). New York: Perennial.

Csikszentmihalyi, M., & Csikszentmihalyi, I. S. (1988). Introduction to Part IV. In M. Csikszentmihalyi & I. S. Csikszentmihalyi (Eds.), *Optimal experience* (pp. 251–265). Cambridge, NY: Cambridge University Press.

Csikszentmihalyi, M., & Hermanson, K. (1995). Intrinsic motivation in museums: What makes visitors want to learn? *Museum News, 74*, 34–61.

Falk, J. H., & Dierking, L. D. (2000). *Learning from museums: Visitor experiences and the making of meaning*. Lanham, MD: Rowman & Littlefield.

Gardner, H. (1993). *Frames of mind: The theory of multiple intelligences* (10th ed.). New York: Basic Books. (Original work published 1983)

Grotzer, T. A. (1996). *Math/science matters: Issues of instructional technique in math and science learning*. Cambridge, MA: Harvard Project on Schooling and Children, Exxon Education Foundation.

Grove, K. (in production). *The Bridges Cohort at Rosa Parks elementary school*. ___:___.

Hein, G. E. (1998). *Learning in the museum*. London: Routledge.

Hooper-Greenhill, E. (1999). *The educational role of the museum*. London: Routledge.

Hektner, J., & Csikszentmihalyi, M. (1996, April). *A longitudinal exploration of flow and intrinsic motivation in adolescents.* Paper presented at the annual meeting of the American Educational Research Association, New York. (ERIC Document Reproduction Service No. ED 395 261)

Jacobs, H. H. (1997). *Mapping the big picture: Integrating curriculum and assessment K–12.* Alexandria, VA: Association for Supervision and Curriculum Development.

Marzano, R. J. (2004). *Building background knowledge for academic achievement: Research on what works in schools.* Alexandria, VA: Association of Supervision and Curriculum Development.

Marzano, R. J., Pickering, D., & McTighe, J. (2000). *Assessing student outcomes: Performance assessment using the dimensions of learning model.* Alexandria, VA: Association of Supervision and Curriculum Development.

Nieto, S. (2003). *Affirming diversity: The sociopolitical context of multicultural education* (4th ed.). Boston: Allyn & Bacon.

Payne, R. (2001). *A framework for understanding poverty* (Rev. ed.). Highlands, TX: Aha Process.

Semper, R. J. (1990). *Science museums as environments for learning.* Retrieved April 1, 2003, from http://www.astc.org.resource/educator/scimus.htm

Strickland, D. S., & Alvermann, D. E. (Eds.). (2004). *Bridging the literacy achievement gap grades 4–12.* New York: Teachers College Press.

Tomlinson, C. A. (2003). *Fulfilling the promise of the differentiated classroom: Strategies and tools for responsive teaching.* Alexandria, VA: Association of Supervision and Curriculum Development.

Torp, L., & Sage, S. (2002). *Problems as possibilities: Problem-based learning for K–12 education* (2nd ed.). Alexandria, VA: Association of Supervision and Curriculum Development.

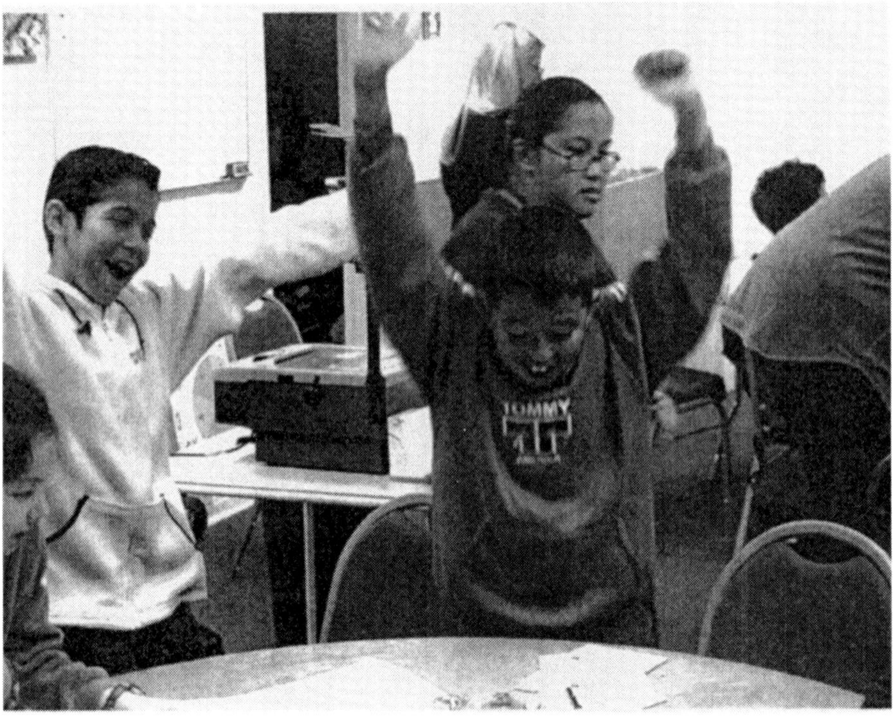
TOMMY

CHAPTER THREE

Talking in Museums: When Vices Turn Into Virtues
Exploring Oral Language Development

Diane Lapp
James Flood

As Larissa recites the features of the modern skull to Andy, he interrupts her to make sure she sees the other skull: "Look, this one is older, the teeth are all grey." Larissa retorts: "Just because it has grey teeth doesn't mean it's old." He considers her remark and says: "Yeah, but the forehead isn't smooth." She replies: "Hmmm . . . and the chin isn't really there and the teeth are different." "Yeah," says Andy, "I bet this one is a million years old." They both laugh.

Exchanges like these among children are common in the School in the Park. These children had just listened to a brief presentation by a museum educator about the anatomy of the skull of modern man. As the presentation was wrapping up, their teacher told them: "Go, explore. See what this museum has to offer." The children scattered to various exhibits and Larissa and Andy found themselves at the same exhibit. Their exchange was informal and decidedly content driven. It shows us how all children can converse with one another when there is something interesting and relevant to talk about; both children were playing the role of archaeologists as they coconstructed meaning. Together, they sorted out meaning; they were able to compare and contrast the two skulls and come to the conclusion that one was the skull of a modern man and the older was the skull of one of the ancestors of modern man.

Their exchange shows the importance of several factors in good conversations:

1. they had something important and relevant to discuss
2. they had the opportunity to talk freely about their observations
3. they had a partner who was listening and speaking
4. their sharing with one another was interactive and social

The *School in the Park Program* fosters oral language growth among the children who participate precisely because it provides the children with numerous opportunities to speak and listen to peers, teachers, museum educators, and knowledgeable adults from all aspects of the park—from the zoo to the aeronautical museum.

HOW ORAL LANGUAGE DEVELOPS

Social interaction significantly affects oral language development (Wells, 1986). In a longitudinal study of British children in England, Wells found that children exposed to the "most" language heard at least 10 times more words than those in home environments with the least amount of language exposure. As you would conclude, researchers found that those who received the most language exposure were also the children who achieved greater school success (Christie, 1985a, 1985b).

Language occurs first in family settings and then in social and classroom contexts. As Vygotsky (1962, 1978), Chomsky (1965), and Bakhtin (1986) noted, language is the primary mediator of learning, and it influences all subsequent social and intellectual development. Researchers working with young children have found that young children who participate in literacy events like "interactive bedtime story" reading develop ability with language, reading, and writing (Adams, 1990; Chaney, 1992; Clay, 1991; Flood, 1977; Teale & Sulzby, 1986).

Based on these findings, you're probably wondering about the type of interaction in schools that would positively affect language learning and oral language development. Researchers have found that the quality of children's oral interactions is a major determinant to their success in school. Children who engaged in one-to-one collaborative interactions with adults; who discussed a shared activity; or who were asked to explain information of interest to a younger listener, developed a greater command of language than their peers who were not engaged in these types of activities (Salus & Flood, 2003). Parents who engaged with children in high-quality interactions provided support that allowed children to intuit nonverbal and verbal cues (Whitehurst & Lonigan, 1998). Children's language flourishes when information that is appropriate to their cognitive and linguistic development is explained and scaffolded (Bruner, 1975, 1983; Whitehurst & Lonigan, 1998).

Entry into school should not be thought of as a beginning, but, rather, it should be thought of as a transition to a more broadly based language community and to a wider range of opportunities for meaning making and mastery of language. Every child has competencies and these provide a positive base from which to start. "The teacher's responsibility is to discover what they are in order to help each child extend and develop them" (Wells, 1986, pp. 68–69). The classroom needs to serve as a social environment that fosters continued language learning because classrooms are critical to children's learning success (Maloch, 2004; Paratore & McCormack, 1998; Pinnell & Jaggar, 2003; Vasquez et al., 2003; Wilkinson & Silliman, 2000). Chomsky described these environments as "places that enable natural curiosity, intelligence, and creativity to develop, and to enable . . . biological capacities to unfold" (Putnam, 1994–1995, p. 331).

This chapter contains examples of School in the Park experiences that will foster the continued language development of students as they learn how to convey the meaning of their thoughts through their interactions with others.

Halliday (1975, pp. 19–21) identified the following seven functions of language used by children as they develop their language skills:

1. *Instrumental:* using language to satisfy personal needs and to get things accomplished
2. *Regulatory:* using language to control the behaviors of others
3. *Personal:* using language to tell about themselves
4. *Interactional:* using language to get along with others
5. *Heuristic:* using language to find out and learn about things
6. *Imaginative:* using language to make believe, to pretend
7. *Informative:* using language to communicate information

Language proficiency develops through interactions that cause children to perform these functions. Learning situations that provide a collaborative, interactive context for language development "invite children to ask, tell, report, discuss, negotiate, test, and direct" (Searfoss, 1988, p. 4).

Here's a quick checklist to assess the current language environment that exists within any classroom. Just answer yes or no to each question:

1. Are teachers initiating all of the classroom conversations?
2. Are you promoting a quiz-like atmosphere of interaction where you ask most of the questions?
3. Are you making all of the requests?

4. Are you always choosing the topics to be discussed?
5. Are you dominating the conversations?

If you answered "Yes" to any of these questions, the language interactions in the classrooms might be encouraging students to offer brief utterances with simple syntax and restricted vocabulary. When asked direct, literal questions, children often focus solely on the answer rather than offering detailed description or elaboration.

Now teachers are probably thinking, "OK, I would love to have one-to-one conversations with each of my students, but I have 30 of them. How is this possible?" Well, have you considered that all of the one-to-one conversations don't need to include the teacher? To explore this possibility, let us share the myriad of language activities that we observed when we visited the School in the Park.

OFF TO THE PARK FOR ORAL LANGUAGE DEVELOPMENT

As described in chapters 1 and 2, each museum becomes the classroom setting and the curriculum theme becomes "the vehicle to teach literacy and develop language" as Judi Bowes, a zoo educator, described it. Credentialed classroom teachers and museum educators work together to ensure that the children's learning is seamless as they transition between the classrooms of the school and museums.

Stop 1: The Museum of Art

Our first stop was at the Museum of Art. Given that our assignment was to critique School in the Park's impact on oral language development, we were keen to observe whether and how the functions of language were developed within the context of various standards-based science and social studies activities. At the Museum of Art we joined third graders who were studying the cultures, traditions, languages, customs, food, architecture, transportation, and religions of the Byzantine Empire (312–1453). The 3-hour integrated lesson included the viewing of a video on Byzantium with a high-spirited discussion about similarities and differences between Byzantium and cultures they've studied, designing mosaic tiles with partner talk, and playing a "commerce" game where they honed their trading skills.

Viewing and Discussing the Video. To prepare the children for the video, Karin Baker (a museum educator) showed pictures of a *minaret* and explained that they would see a tower (a minaret) in the video that was attached to the mosque, indicating that it was a place for Muslims to worship. One child asked if this would be like "a cross for Christians" and another added "or a Star of David for Jews." After the video the children participated in a freewheeling discussion about their reactions to what they saw.

Ms. Baker then showed them several artifacts (carpets, cloth, bowls) while asking them if these could have come from an ancient ruin. The children discussed the possibilities and their rationales for their decisions. During this experience children used language *heuristically* and *informatively* while the teacher assumed the roles of facilitator, participant, mediator, and active listener. These are the common roles that teachers engage in when they design a curriculum that promotes student conversation as a means to learn new information *and* to develop language skills (Short, Kauffman, Kaser, Kahn, & Crawford, 1999).

Designing Mosaic Tiles. Each child was invited to create a Byzantine tile with designs that illustrated the symmetrical art designs of the Byzantine Empire. To prepare for this experience the teacher shared and discussed the art and icons of this period. As the children crafted their tiles they were engaged in partner talk that involved many language functions, such as *Instrumental*: "I need the white paint"; *Personal*: "Yours is so pretty," gasped Loretta when David held his up for her to see; *Regulatory*: "No, first do inside (paint) the circle"; and *Imaginative*: "Look, mine looks like fire coming out."

During this experience the teachers acted as mediators as they conversed with children and encouraged them to connect the art on their tiles to what they had viewed and learned about Byzantine art.

Creating a Log and Playing the "Commerce" Game. To prepare for this 6,000-mile journey from Chang'an, China, to the great western city of Byzantium the children explored the museum's collection of Asian art, discussed the unique architecture, cultures, and customs of the people they would meet on their journey. They studied maps to gain familiarity with the topography and climates they would encounter.

Their discussions involved hypothesizing what it would be like to take this journey on Bactrian camels that they created as a 3-D sculpture, and how they would need to trade their silk for goods and services in Chang'an, Kashgar, Baghdad, and Tyre if they were to survive their journey. As teams, they became the merchants of each of these cities and played a trading game that engaged them in bartering, and later in discussing the complexities of fair trade practices.

Lively conversation ensued as they played the "commerce" game. The conversation was to the point: let's get what we need to survive the journey. As they figured out what they needed they roamed to other tables to see if they could barter their goods for the goods they needed:

> Angel: I was just counting to be sure.
>
> Javi: She dropped two spices. Oh no, we'll never make it to Tyre.
>
> Martin: We got 100 golds and give it all to me.
>
> Jesse: Go to Byzantium. Hurry.
>
> Javi: I'm supposed to be going to Tyre.
>
> Martin: I'll trade you 1 camel, 2 spices, and 1 gold for a boat. OK?
>
> Angel: No way. No, no, no, no, no we only have one.
>
> Javi: Oh no, you messed me up.

Angel, Martin, and Javi all "high fived" each other.

All of the information and insights they gained were collected by them in their individual passport journals complete with their photo. After several "grand discussions" where they employed all of the functions of language, they composed reflective personal statements highlighting the complexities of trade. As they shared their insights of being "suckered" and not counting their money well enough, they munched on the fruits of each country. The teachers' roles were deliberately fluid as they joined the conversations and discussions, answering questions, adding needed bits of information, supporting, applauding, and encouraging, while trying to very strategically make grade-level study engaging, comfortable, motivating, child centered, and self-evaluative as children explored topical information through good discussions, reading, and writing activities. These were exemplary teachers or as Block, Oakar, and Hurt (2002) described them "master guardians, catching, cradling, and championing every child's discoveries about print" (p. 189) and the many nuances and functions of language.

Stop 2: The Historical Museum

"What will the world be like in 2099?" This was the first question we heard the museum educator, Kim Vukasovich, ask another group of third graders whose classroom had become The Historical Museum. Believe it or not, this futuristic probe was an introduction to the study of the Kumeyaay Indians, which is part of the required third-grade California History Standards. As students contemplated a response, the museum instructor invited them to scientifically support their hypotheses and then to share their thoughts with a partner. She then introduced several historical Kumeyaay Indian artifacts and invited the children to hypothesize what they were and how they had been used. She prompted them to consider the physical properties of color, shape, size, smell, and sound, and to relate these to the needs of people.

Prior to our joining the group they had discussed the Kumeyaay culture, traditions, art, religion, language, customs, and values. After their discussions about the functional possibilities of the artifacts, the children, who were assigned to small groups, viewed photographs and discussed which component of the Kumeyaay culture was shown in each. Several of the photographs illustrated the complexities of basket weaving, a skill that had been passed down through generations of Kumeyaay. After much group discussion the children presented the photographs sequentially to illustrate the process.

This learning situation invited the children to observe, examine, and compare as they participated in carefully crafted state standards-based curriculum codesigned by their teachers. Student conversations illustrated their reasoning as well as their internalization of the functions of language and conversation.

Their patterns of discourse were unrestricted as the instructional stance of their classroom teacher and museum instructor was that of facilitators. The students' content knowledge was shaped as they used language for many purposes, in many situations, and with varied audiences (Barnes, 1972), during this week of study.

Stop 3: The Museum of Man

Our next visit was to the Museum of Man where fourth graders were viewing a human skeleton and engaging in an interactive discussion about the parts of their bodies as a segment of their study of evolution. Words like mandible, cranium, sternum, and patella were used by the children as they questioned the museum educator Amy Whitman about the intricacies of their bodies. She in turn invited them to consider what would happen to their bodies if their spinal cord were severed. As the children pondered this, their conversation involved explanations, personal experiences, descriptions, additional questions, and elaborations that changed the focus from being primarily teacher initiated to a very child-centered exchange that involved the children in all of the language functions.

During these student-initiated conversations the Rosa Parks teachers stayed on the sidelines, but, like the exemplary teachers described by Pressley et al. (2001), they were making a difference in the literacy lives of their students by ensuring that students connected to each other's comments and ideas. They also actively joined the discussions, at times modeling appropriate conversational strategies like turn taking, active listening, polite questioning, and scaffolded reasoned responses. After these conversations the children and the museum educator took turns as leader of "Simon Says" to reinforce their knowledge of the technical words that represent parts of their bodies, for example, "Simon Says touch your cranium. Touch your sternum."

Next they explored the museum's *Footsteps Through Time Exhibit* where they observed and discussed the environment, anatomy, and behavior of primates with teachers and peers.

During this week-long study they viewed films and exhibits, discussed, hypothesized, contrasted ideas, presented, and engaged in language experiences that expanded their understandings of ancient civilizations. Their classroom talk was unlike a "series of scripts" that are often played out in classrooms (Hatch, 1992; Padak, 1986). Instead, as Platt (1984) described, the functions of language they used varied according to the situation and dimension of the rich contexts and content they were exploring at any given time.

Stop 4: Junior Theater

A second group of fourth-grade students engaged in meaningful discussions as they prepared for a performance at the Junior Theatre. A study of the Gold Rush, required curriculum in the State of California, allowed the museum educators and the credentialed teachers to weave performance into a standards-based, content-appropriate curriculum. As the children ran through their rehearsals, it became clear that their understanding of the Gold Rush expanded as they took on the parts of the characters who "rushed" to California in 1849 hoping for a better life. The children laughed with delight as they rehearsed their scene in which Marta exclaims "Eureka! We found gold in the hills!"

The children's conversations and performance illustrated their understanding of the significant roles played by people like James Marshall and John Sutter, the conflicts of warring cultures, as well as the trials of people hoping for advancement. The insights and wonderings of these young children during their table talk conversations reinforced our belief that children of poverty exhibit higher achievement when they have classroom experiences that promote meaning-based learning (Knapp, 1995). Jaime, for example, said, "Did the people moving west have the right to pan for the gold? Was it on the Indians' land?" Kim said, "I think this is why the Native Americans were fighting them." Joseph noted, "Native Americans still don't live near White people, they don't trust them." As we observed these interchanges we realized that we were viewing what Lindfors (1999, p. 3) referred to as "the seamless union of four aspects of language: communication purpose or intention, expression (of purpose, of content, of stance), participants, and context" in a setting prompted by wonderings, information seeking, investigation, inquiry, and conversation. These students were freely exchanging ideas because their teachers had designed curricula that invited them to assume responsibility for their learning.

As the children dressed in their costumes, they took on the lives of prospectors of 1849 and they grew in their appreciation of the content they were learning. They had become the 49ers.

Their conversations about the lives of the 49ers continued as they watched the videotape of their own performances. Not only did they critique their own performance with comments like "I messed up on that word," "I smiled at exactly the right moment," "Wow, I was loud enough," but they also added content information that they had learned "I should have said that stuff about how John Sutter helped the people who had come from New York."

Stop 5: Aerospace Museum

"Do you think we need to add more tissue for protection?" "Let's try it to see." "Be sure to tape it tightly or it will come apart." "I want to drop it this time." "If we don't get it right our astronaut will die." " I'd like to be an astronaut." "You'd be good, but I'd be scared. Sometimes they crash." This conversation was shared by a group of fifth graders at the Aerospace Museum as they prepared a hot air balloon drop that simulated dropping an astronaut from a space retrieval system. As illustrated by their table talk they were using all of the functions of language. Many of these children had been involved in School in the Park experiences for 3 years so their table talk was on topic and elaborate, affirming the belief that the visual arts and literacy arts can form a complementary partnership in meaning-based curriculum (Carger, 2004; Short, Kauffman, & Kahn, 2000).

Once the children had completed the drop, they discussed the whys of their success or the changes that should be made before they were ready for another drop. They prepared group reports, which depicted the process and their reflections.

Prior to the presentation the children discussed the characteristics of a successful presentation with their classroom teacher. Their oral and written discourses overlapped because they were so natural and well integrated within the participation requirements generated by this curriculum context. The children practiced their presentations before they went before their peers. The children illustrated in this photo were making sure that their voices carried so that their classmates could hear them clearly.

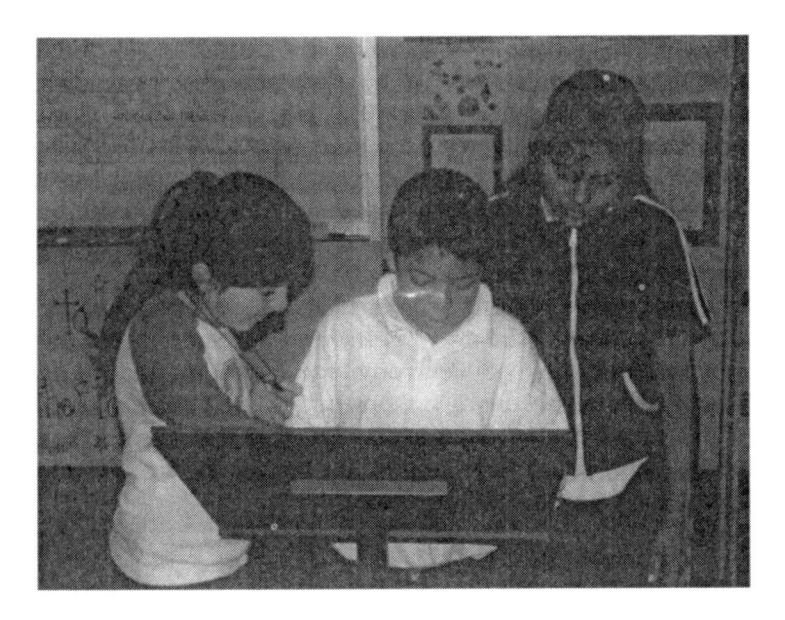

Children practicing for their oral presentations.

Stop 6: The Hall of Champions

A fantasy baseball scavenger hunt was a partner experience for a second group of fifth graders at the Hall of Champions Museum. As they sought answers to questions like "Who currently owns the Padres?" "When is the Golden Glove awarded?" "What are four facts about Ted Williams?" they maneuvered each other through walls of information to search for titles or clue words that would help them be the first to find their answers. Their dialogue reflected their awe of the accomplishments of these champions. Their "real" language was occurring because of engagement in a "real" setting (Booth, 1991; Wallach, 1990).

Stop 7: San Diego Zoo

"Today was my best day because I saw so much and had so much to write in my journal." This was a statement made to a friend by a fifth grader after exploring a bird aviary at the San Diego Zoo. Students took notes and recorded the characteristics of the various birds they were observing. They were encouraged by the museum instructor, who was also a credentialed teacher, to compare and contrast what they were learning about these animals with other animals they had studied. The children accepted this challenge, and we later heard Tomas tell his partner that the bird they were observing reminded him of Kumeyaay birds they had earlier studied.

Children and teacher sharing questions and conversation.

Judi Bowes, zoo educator, asked them "This is a bird of prey. Does that mean that it is devout?" "No," responded Daniel. "I learned about owls on the Discovery channel. It means they hunt other animals to use for their food source." The children were delighted in all of their discoveries and also that the next day they were going to dissect owl pellets and pet a cockroach as they studied invertebrates. This week provided them with multiple opportunities to engage in dialogues where they could easily practice the functions of language while acquiring standards-based content.

When the children were introduced to Emily, the beautiful owl in the picture, they were filled with questions and observations: "How big is the biggest animal she ate? Look, Rosio, she can turn her head almost all the way around." The zoo instructor was delighted with their questions and observations, and allowed the children to closely examine Emily, who seemed oblivious to their amazement.

CONCLUSION

Engagement of learners through oral discourse that is connected to content and literacy learning occurred in each museum classroom that we visited through conversational discussion groups. Back in their Rosa Parks classrooms all of these conversations continued as their teachers used computer-based technologies to promote literacy and content knowledge

(Reinking, 1998). The curricular experiences designed by these teachers demonstrated their belief that language and literacy development "is not a state of grace that one arrives at. Rather it is continuously learning, becoming, and experiencing literacy across time and space" (Prentiss, 1998, p. 124).

Could these experiences happen inside a school-based classroom? Although the City Heights teachers have taken advantage of the city in which they live, experiences like these can occur in other cities where teachers use multiple contexts such as the local resources, film, literature, and the Internet to broaden the world of the classroom and engage their students. For many urban children the experiences provided by the school are their primary literacy experiences (Lapp, Fisher, Flood, & Moore, 2002). Engaged learners in any situation master knowledge when their classrooms are organized around motivating content (Almasi & McKeown, 1996). The importance of motivation as a major engagement factor in learning is highlighted in the work of Guthrie and Alvermann (1999). The School in the Park is a model that exemplifies the importance of the "engagement" where children are actively learning while integrating language and literacy learning across all areas of the curriculum. Policies are needed that guarantee engaged learning for every child. School in the Park provides a context necessary to promote and foster language development. Creating a rich context for oral language is the responsibility of educators and absolutely essential for children who may have reduced exposure to varied and sophisticated language outside of school. The reality of such a guarantee lay within a collective educational response that can occur through the efforts of each teacher and administrator as we answer the question, "What can I be doing in my classroom, school, or community to make this a mainstay of public education?"

With programs like "The School in the Park," we believe children can blossom as language learners and language users. We fully concur with Virginia Satir (1967) when she said: "Feelings of worth can flourish only in an atmosphere where individual differences are appreciated, mistakes are tolerated, communication is open, and rules are flexible—the kind of atmosphere that is found in a nurturing family" (p. 3).

REFERENCES

Adams, M. J. (1990). *Beginning to read: Thinking and learning about print*. Cambridge, MA: MIT Press.

Almasi, J., & McKeown, M. (1996). The nature of engaged reading in classroom discussions of literature. *Journal of Literacy Research, 28*, 107–146.

Bakhtin, M. M. (1986). *Speech genres and other late essays* (C. Emerson & M. Holquist, Eds.; V. W. McGee, Trans.). Austin, TX: University of Texas Press.

Barnes, D. (1972). Language and learning in the classroom. In *Language in education: A sourcebook* (pp. 112–118). London: Routledge & Kegan Paul, in association with Open University Press.

Block, C., Oakar, M., & Hurt, N. (2002). The expertise of literacy teachers: A continuum from preschool to grade 5. *Reading Research Quarterly, 37,* 178–207.

Booth, D. (1991). "Imaginary gardens with real toads." Reading and drama in education. *Theory Into Practice, 24,* 193–198.

Bruner, J. (1975). Language as an instrument of thought. In A. Davies (Ed.), *Problems of language and learning* (pp. 61–81). London: Heinemann.

Bruner, J. S. (1983). *Children's talk: Learning to use language.* London: Norton.

Carger, C. L. (2004). Art and literacy with bilingual children. *Language Arts, 81,* 283–292.

Chaney, C. (1992). Language development, metalinguistic skills, and print awareness in 3-year-old children. *Applied Psycholinguistics, 13,* 485–514.

Chomsky, N. A. (1965). *Aspects of the theory of syntax.* Cambridge, MA: MIT Press.

Christie, F. (1985a). Language and schooling. In S. N. Tchudi (Ed.), *Language, schooling, and society* (pp. 21–40). Montclair, NJ: Boynton/Cook.

Christie, F. (1985b). *Language education.* Victoria, Australia: Deakin University.

Clay, M. M. (1991). *Becoming literate: The construction of inner control.* Portsmouth, NH: Heinemann.

Flood, J. (1977). Parental styles in reading episodes with young children. *The Reading Teacher, 30,* 864–867.

Guthrie, J., & Alvermann, D. (Eds.). (1999). *Engaged reading: Processes, practices, and policy implications.* New York: Teachers College Press.

Halliday, M. A. K. (1975). *Learning how to mean: Exploration in the development of language.* London: Edward Arnold.

Hatch, E. (1992). *Discourse and language education.* New York: Cambridge University Press.

Knapp, M. (1995). *Teaching for meaning in high-poverty classrooms.* New York: Teachers College Press.

Lapp, D., Fisher, D., Flood, J., & Moore, K. (2002). "I don't want to teach it wrong": An investigation of the role families believe they should play in the early literacy development of their children. *Yearbook of the National Reading Conference, 51,* 275–286.

Lindfors, J. (1999). *Children's inquiry: Using language to make sense of the world.* New York: Teachers College Press, Language and Literacy Series.

Maloch, B. (2004). One teacher's journey: Transitioning into literature discussion groups. *Language Arts, 81,* 313–322.

Padak, N. (1986). Teachers' verbal behaviors: A window to the teaching process. *Yearbook of The National Reading Conference, 35,* 185–191.

Paratore, J. R., & McCormack, R. L. (Eds.). (1998). *Peer talk in the classroom.* Newark, DE: International Reading Association.

Pinnell, G. S., & Jaggar, A. M. (2003). Oral language: Speaking and listening in elementary classrooms. In J. Flood, D. Lapp, J. Squire, & J. Jensen (Eds.), *Handbook of research on teaching the English language arts* (2nd ed., pp. 881–913). Mahwah, NJ: Lawrence Erlbaum Associates.

Platt, N. G. (1984). How one classroom gives access to meaning. *Theory Into Practice, 23,* 239–245.

Prentiss, T. (1998). Teachers and students mutually influence each other's literacy practices: A focus on the student's role. In D. A. Alvermann, K. A. Hinchman, D. W. Moore, S. F. Phelps, & D. R. Waff (Eds.), *Reconceptualizing the literacies in adolescents' lives* (pp. 103–128). Mahwah, NJ: Lawrence Erlbaum Associates.

Pressley, M., Wharton-McDonald, R., Allington, R., Block, C. C., Morrow, L., Tracey, D., Baker, K., Brooks, G., Cronin, J., Nelson, E., & Woo, D. (2001). A study of effective grade 1 reading instruction. *Scientific Studies of Reading, 5,* 35–58.

Putnam, L. R. (1994–1995). An interview with Noam Chomsky. *The Reading Teacher, 48,* 328–333.

Reinking, D. (1998). Introduction: Synthesizing technological transformations of literacy in a post-typographic world. In D. Reinking, C. McKenna, L. Labbo, & R. Kieffer (Eds.), *Handbook of literacy and technology: Transformations in a post-typographical world* (pp. xi–xxx). Mahwah, NJ: Lawrence Erlbaum Associates.

Salus, P., & Flood, J. (2003). *Language: A user's guide—What we say and why.* San Diego, CA: Academic Professional Development.

Satir, V. (1967). *Conjoint family therapy: A guide to theory and technique.* Palo Alto, CA: Science and Behavior Books.

Searfoss, L. W. (1988). Winds of change in reading instruction. *Reading Instruction Journal, 31*(1), 2–6.

Short, K. G., Kauffman, G., & Kahn, L. H. (2000). "I just need to draw." Responding to literature across multiple sign systems. *The Reading Teacher, 54,* 160–171.

Short, K., Kauffman, G., Kaser, S., Kahn, L., & Crawford, K. (1999). Teacher watching: Examining teacher talk in literature circles. *Language Arts, 76,* 377–385.

Teale, W., & Sulzby, E. (Eds.). (1986). *Emergent literacy: Writing and reading.* Norwood, NJ: Ablex.

Vasquez, V., Muise, M., Adamson, S., Heffernan, L., Chiola-Nakai, D., & Shear, J. (2003). *Getting beyond "I like the book": Creating space for critical literacy in K–6 classrooms.* Newark, DE: International Reading Association.

Vygotsky, L. (1962). *Thought and language.* Cambridge, MA: MIT Press.

Vygotsky, L. (1978). *Mind in society: The development of higher psychological processes* (M. Cole, V. John-Steiner, S. Scribner, & E. Souberman, Trans.). Cambridge, MA: Harvard University Press.

Wallach, G. (1990). Magic buries Celtics: Looking for broader interpretations of language learning and literacy. *Topics in Language Disorders, 10*(2), 63–80.

Wells, G. (1986). *The meaning makers: Children learning language and using language to learn.* Portsmouth, NH: Heinemann.

Whitehurst, G., & Lonigan, C. (1998). Child development and emergent literacy. *Child Development, 69,* 848–872.

Wilkinson, I., & Silliman, E. (2000). Classroom language and literacy learning. In M. Kamil, P. Mosenthal, P. D. Pearson, & R. Barr (Eds.), *Handbook of reading research* (Vol. III, pp. 337–360). Mahwah, NJ: Lawrence Erlbaum Associates.

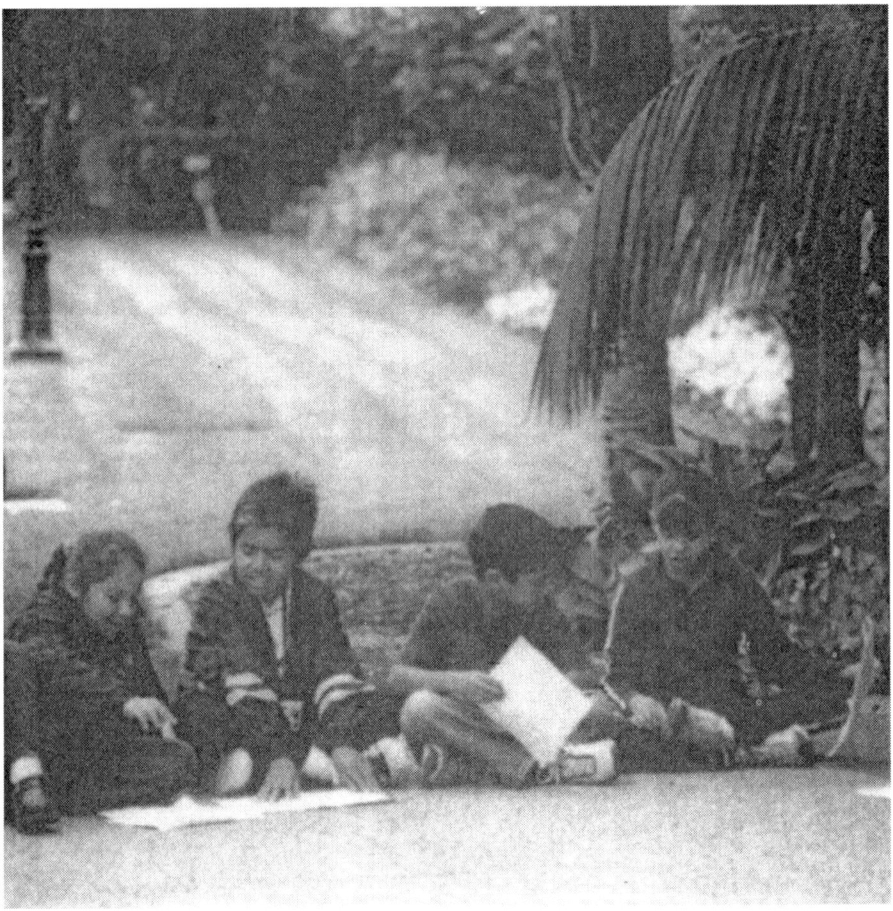

CHAPTER FOUR

Reading in the Park

Nancy Frey

It's a beautiful spring morning and the Reading Is Fundamental (RIF) book giveaway is in full swing. For the last 90 minutes, teachers at Rosa Parks Elementary have been bringing their students to view and choose books to take home. Colleen Crandall's fourth-grade class approaches the tables that have been set up in the school's courtyard. While many of the children locate books of interest, one student continues to search. Because I have been volunteering at the tables all morning, I am confident I know all the books available. "What kind of book are you looking for?" I offer. The young girl continues to move books aside to view all the titles, then looks up at me with a hopeful expression. "Do you have any books on the Muses? I'm interested in the Muses. We did a play at School in the Park and I want to read more about them."

I was not able to find a book on the Muses that morning for Dulce (I later found Aliki's [1997] *The Gods and Goddesses of Olympus*), but I cannot recall a more telling example of the influence of the School in the Park program on the reading of its participants. Dulce's experience at the Museum of Photographic Arts (MOPA) had included production of the Greek myth *Orpheus and Eurydice*. She explained that Orpheus, son of the muse Calliope, lost his true love when he failed to obey Pluto's warning to not look back over his shoulder as he and his wife were leaving Hades. Dulce was also interested in two of Calliope's sisters, familiar now to her as the masks representing comedy and drama. Something about the notion of the muses had piqued her interest and she was now determined to find out more about them. I couldn't fail to appreciate that the word "museum" is derived from the name of the temple of these daughters of Zeus who inspired learning in the arts and sciences. Indeed, such a shrine was ensconced in every school in ancient Greece to call on the muses to inspire learners. In San Diego, school and museum are once again intertwined in Balboa Park. I was asked to visit School in the Park and critique it from the perspective of reading instruction.

A Focus on Standards

A core principle of the School in the Park (SITP) program is that students experience a standards-based core curriculum taught using research-based instructional practices. Throughout this chapter you will notice references to curricular and professional standards. I have used the McREL Language Arts Standards and Benchmarks for K to 12 Education to cite curricular standards. The professional standards used are the National Board of Professional Teaching Standards (NBPTS), developed jointly by the International Reading Association and the organization that certifies candidates for National Board certification. Those cited are derived from the standards for early and middle childhood/literacy Reading–Language Arts.

What Is Reading?

At its most basic level, reading is the act of understanding written language. However, this act requires a complex interaction involving the skills of decoding, vocabulary knowledge, and fluency, as well as comprehension strategies to make meaning of the text (Samuels & Kamil, 1984). The ability to perform these tasks is further influenced by motivation, prior knowledge, and language proficiency (Snow, Burns, & Griffin, 1998). The result is a transaction between the text and the reader that produces a unique response in the mind of the reader (Rosenblatt, 1978).

Reading is one aspect of literacy development, along with writing, speaking, listening, and viewing (Harris & Hodges, 1995). These processes interface to foster mutual development of all the aspects of language. In fact, this interaction of written, oral, and visual processes is considered critical for effective reading instruction (Armbruster & Osborn, 2002). Therefore, although this chapter addresses reading, it is inexorably bound in other literacy practices. Discussions of writing can be found in Fearn and Farnan's chapter in this book, and oral language development is examined in detail in the chapter by Lapp and Flood.

Because School in the Park is designed to "integrate formal education experience with more informal museum-based experiences," a discussion of the reading program at school is in order (Spencer, 2002, p. 2). Reading instruction at Rosa Parks is delivered in a daily 3-hour literacy block based on the gradual release of responsibility model (Pearson & Fielding, 1991). Each day teachers foster reading acquisition through the instructional practices of read alouds, shared reading, guided reading, and independent reading (Frey & Fisher, 2006). In addition, students write for purpose each day through a process of intentional writing instruction (Fearn & Farnan, 2001). Learners also participate in anchored word instruction that emphasizes sound–letter relationships, vocabulary development, and word analysis (Bear, Invernizzi, Templeton, & Johnston, 2004; Juel, Biancarosa, Coker, & Deffes, 2003). A summary of the literacy block and its research base is presented in Fig. 4.1.

Although fourth- and fifth-grade students also attend School in the Park, I have chosen to highlight the third-grade experience. During the

Instructional Practice	What Is It?	What Is the Research Base?
Read alouds	Students hear text above their independent level from a fluent language model	Fisher, Flood, Lapp, & Frey, 2004 Ivey & Broaddus, 2001
Shared reading	Students have access to a text while teacher models comprehension strategies	Allen, 2002 Holdaway, 1979
Guided reading and literature circles	Students read leveled text while teacher coaches and scaffolds	Daniels, 2002 Fountas & Pinnell, 2001
Independent reading	Students read texts of their own choosing or from a range of teacher-selected books	Pilgreen, 2000 Stanovich, 1986
Writing instruction	Students are taught mechanics, conventions, craft, modes of discourse, and processes of writing	Fearn & Farnan, 2001 Fisher & Frey, 2003
Anchored word study	Students learn sound–symbol relationships, vocabulary, spelling, and word analysis	Bear, Invernizzi, Templeton, & Johnston, 2004 Juel, Biancarosa, Coker, & Deffes, 2003

FIG. 4.1. The literacy block.

year, third-grade students visit three museums—the San Diego Zoo, the San Diego Art Museum, and the San Diego Historical Society. This chapter provides a snapshot of reading experiences encountered by the third graders during the course of their first year at SITP.

How Is Reading Taught in School in the Park?

The focus on reading instruction during School in the Park is on building background knowledge and cultivating a sense of inquiry in order to make texts meaningful. While at the museums, students do not participate in the traditional reading instruction discussed in the previous section. Rather, they use a variety of texts, diagrams, graphs, maps, and environmental print to gather information and provoke their intellectual wonderings. Student motivation to read is built in because they *must* read in order to satisfy their curiosities about the biological, artistic, and historical worlds they are entering each time they set foot in a museum. The goal is not to replicate classroom instruction, but rather to connect reading to the world beyond the classroom.

Reading the World

Brazilian educational philosopher Paulo Freire observed that in order to read words we must be able to read the world described by those words (Freire & Macedo, 1987). This world knowledge is acquired through meaningful experiences that relate to the learner's life, which then transfer to reading of the printed word. When the learner has a high level of background knowledge concerning the content of the reading, he or she is able to read more complex text. A study of young adults with low reading levels found that when the text selections focused on familiar topics they were able to comprehend five grade levels above their tested general reading levels (Sticht, 1988–1989).

Reading the world is a continual process built on three conditions: perception, inquiry, and reflection (Freire & Macedo, 1987). The students attending School in the Park develop their ability to read the world through experiences designed to expose them to new views (perception), promote curiosity through intriguing questions (inquiry), and allowing time to consider what they need to learn next (reflection). Dulce's search for a book about muses was evidence of her reflection on her learning experience at MOPA, for she had turned to the word in order to understand the world. (McREL LA.7.II.6. Uses prior knowledge and experience to understand and respond to new information.)

READING IN THREE WORLDS: BIOLOGICAL, ARTISTIC, AND HISTORICAL

Reading the Biological World

Perception. Roberta Dawson's third-grade students spent a rare rainy morning at the San Diego Zoo searching for animals that had adapted to their environment in order to survive. Led by museum educator Judi Bowes and their classroom teacher, students observed two polar bears swim and play. While the children crowded around the glass walls to get a closer look, the museum educator asked them to determine the color of the polar bear's skin. Students initially suggested that it might be pink or white, only to be reminded to look for places on the polar bear where the skin was exposed. Soon the children noticed that the bears' noses and footpads were black. Could the polar bears' skin be black all over? Students used the details of their visual observation to formulate a conclusion about a physical characteristic of the bears. (McREL SC.12.II. 3. Plans and conducts simple investigations.)

Inquiry. Learning a simple fact about the color of a polar bear's skin was not the goal of the lesson. The museum educator and the teacher challenged students to apply their newly acquired knowledge to formulate a series of questions. (NBPTS RLA.VII. Reading teachers encourage student self-assessment and gather information to report to various audiences.) Why would the skin be black? Several students made a connection between heat absorption and black surfaces, prompting a lively discussion about black cars on sunny days. She explained that the black skin allows the bear to absorb the light from the Arctic sun, generating heat that keeps the bear warm.

This provoked another series of questions about the bears. After all, if the bears' coat is white, how could sunlight penetrate the heavy fur to reach the black skin? Now the most surprising fact of all was revealed—polar bears are not white. The shafts of hair are transparent, allowing light to penetrate to the surface of the skin. The lack of pigment in the hair shaft allows the light to be refracted so that it appears white. This important adaptation also allows the bear to blend in to its natural environment of ice and snow, making it a more effective hunter.

Armed with this background information, students now jockeyed for position around the large plaques displaying written information about polar bears. As in Sticht's findings, these 8-year-olds were able to read complex text written above their independent reading levels because they possessed a higher level of knowledge about the topic. (McREL LA.7.II.1. Uses reading skills and strategies to understand a variety of informational texts.) Words like "adaptation" were comprehensible because they had participated in inquiry learning to build background knowledge before reading text. (McREL LA.5.II.4. Uses phonetic and structural analysis techniques, syntactic structure, and semantic context to decode unknown words.)

Reflection. The learning on biological adaptation did not end with the visit to the polar bear installation. Their teacher read aloud books on polar bears and on animal adaptations to bridge her students' knowledge of the world with information found on the printed page and made other books available for independent reading. (NBPTS RLA.VIII. Integration of literacy processes across curriculum.) A list of these titles can be found in Fig. 4.2.

Led by the teacher and museum educator, students synthesized their understanding about biological adaptations by creating accordion books chronicling their learning. After constructing the books, students chose pictures of animals they had studied to affix to the left page and wrote about the animal's adaptation to its environment on the right page. These student-created books later became part of the class library of original texts to be read and shared by all. (McREL LA.4.II.8. Uses strategies to compile information into written reports or summaries.)

Constructing Meaning Through Reader Response

Another element of reading instruction is reader response to text. Rosenblatt (1978) defined this as a transaction between reader and text that is influenced by both what the writer has written and what the reader has experienced. These responses can be conceptualized on a continuum from efferent (cognitive) to aesthetic (affective):

> In the efferent reading, attention is focused predominantly on abstracting out, analyzing, and structuring what is to be retained after the reading, e.g.,

---

Books on Biological Adaptation

Crow, S. L. (1985). *Penguins and polar bears: Animals of the ice and snow.* Washington, DC: National Geographic Society.

Ganeri, A. (1997). *Creature features: How it works.* New York: Simon & Schuster.

Kalman, B. (2000). *How do animals adapt? The science of living things.* New York: Crabtree.

Kirschner, D. S. (2001). *Reptiles and amphibians: My first pocket guide.* Washington, DC: National Geographic Society.

Oliver, N. (1994). *Best beak in Boonaroo Bay.* Melbourne, Australia: Lothian.

Parker, H. (1999). *Fantastic animal features.* Austin, TX: Steck-Vaughn.

FIG. 4.2. Books for biological adaptation unit.

factual information or analysis. In an aesthetic reading, attention is focused predominantly on what is being lived through during the reading, the ideas and feelings being evoked and organized as the work corresponding to the text. This evocation constitutes the work that is the object of interpretation and evaluation. (Rosenblatt, 2003, p. 70)

These responses should not be viewed solely at the edges, with informational text at one extreme and poems at the other. Rather, the response is likely to be multifaceted and can be situated anywhere on the continuum because the reader can analyze facts and feel the emotions concurrently. At School in the Park, students have many opportunities to experience both the efferent and aesthetic responses to a different kind of text. In other words, students' responses can be elicited through significant works of art or nature.

Reading the Artistic World

Perception. Kate Anderson-Gray's third-grade students spent time in the San Diego Museum of Art learning how to read a painting. (NBPTS RLA. XII. Reading teachers use a wide variety of print and non-print resources to develop students' viewing and visual representation.) Museum educator Karin Baker used the site's large collection of Italian Renaissance paintings to teach the "vocabulary" artists employ to tell a story with line, shape, color, form, and texture in the same way authors use words to describe. (McREL LA.9.II.1. Understands different messages conveyed through visual media [e.g., main ideas and supporting details; facts and opinions; main characters, setting, and sequence of events in visual narratives].) They began by viewing paintings from the period to note the settings, especially the architecture of the time and the absence of modern inventions like automobiles. The museum educator and teacher asked students to describe how they felt as they looked at each painting, then connected the artistic vocabulary to their words by pointing out the use of these elements. Later, Ms. Anderson-Gray equated these landscapes to the descriptive passages used by authors to create settings for their stories. (NBPTS RLA. IX. Reading teachers use their knowledge of reading processes, language development, texts, and ongoing assessment to advance literacy and develop strategic readers.)

Students then moved on to narrative paintings created during the Italian Renaissance. One work by Veronese called *Apollo and Daphne* (oil on canvas, c. 1565–1570) is a narrative painting depicting the nymph Daphne's transformation into a tree to save her from Apollo. The museum educator and the teacher lead a discussion on how the story can be discerned by the details in the painting. In particular, they observed how Daphne's hands and feet were taking on the appearance of tree limbs and roots and predicted how the painting would be different if it had been painted minutes or hours earlier or later. The concept of prediction is not only a skill used by good readers; Ms. Gray-Anderson would not miss the opportunity to use this predictive art lesson as background knowledge when she discussed prediction as part of the literacy instruction block back at school.

Inquiry. Students then moved through the large spaces of the museum to view portraits from the period like *Portrait of a Young Man* by Giorgione (oil on panel, c. 1510), and to discuss the artist's use of dark background and close perspective to emphasize the subject's intense gaze. In contrast, *Portrait of a Florentine Noblewoman* (artist unknown, c. 1540) features details in her dress and setting that represent her opulent lifestyle. Students were then asked to discuss their answers to a series of efferent and aesthetic questions and furnish evidence to support their positions. (NBPTS RLA. XI. Reading teachers provide opportunities for students to listen and speak for a variety of purposes and audiences.)

- What can you say about the person in the painting?
- How do you know if they were wealthy or poor?
- Why were they painted?
- How do you feel when you look at the person in the painting?

These questions provoked spirited conversation and ideas among students, who used a variety of details, including clothing, setting, and the titles of the paintings in their replies. (McREL LA.9.II.4. Understands the different ways in which people are stereotyped in visual media and understands that people could have been represented differently.) The strategies used by students to read the narratives of paintings corresponded to those used for "making inferences" another essential reading comprehension skill.

Reflection. Working in groups of four, students collaborated to create a series of narrative paintings about a fictional character named Giuseppe who lived in Florence at the time of the Renaissance. Each group received an information sheet with background information on Giuseppe's life at the age of 8, 15, or 25. A fourth group read about his trip to Venice. Using the information gleaned from the biographical reading, students created a series of narrative paintings on 22" × 28" stock to tell the story of Giuseppe. (McREL LA.7.II.1. Uses reading skills and strategies to understand a variety of informational texts.) They applied what they had learned about setting, especially architecture, topography, and clothing to include in the details of the painting. As well, they needed to convey his physical characteristics and emotions at the time of the portrait. The resulting series of paintings could be read as a sequence story of the life of Giuseppe of Florence.

Students continued to apply their experiences at the Museum of Art to their reading for the remainder of the school year. Observations about landscapes linked to their connections about the settings of stories they read during the literacy block and in their science and social studies classes. (McREL LA.6.II.14.1. Understands differences in literary works in terms of settings.) The portraits served as a metaphor for the biographical study they completed through literature circles and guided reading back at Rosa Parks. (McREL LA.6.II.5. Understands elements of character development in literary works.) Roberta Dawson's class read a series of biographies about notable artists, some of whom they viewed in the museum. (McREL LA.6.II.1. Uses reading skills and strategies to understand a variety of literary passages and texts.) Figure 4.3 features a list of picture book biographies on artists, a suitable medium for the topic.

Creating Meaning Through Strategic Reading

In order for students to read and comprehend text, they need skills, the "information-processing techniques that are automatic" such as decoding and fluency (Paris, Wasik, & Turner, 1991). They also need a set of strategies they can access to make meaning of more difficult text. These strategies are tools the learner conscientiously activates to support their own comprehension. Paris et al. (1991) stress six reasons for teaching reading strategies:

- Organization and evaluation of concepts in the text
- Development of other cognitive strategies like memory and attention
- Controlled by the reader

Artist Biographies in Third Grade

Anholt, L. (1996). *Degas and the little dancer.* Hauppauge, NY: Barrons.
Bjork, C. (1987). *Linnea in Monet's garden.* New York: Farrar, Straus & Giroux.
Laden, N. (1998). *When Pigasso met Mootise.* San Francisco: Chronicle.
Mayhew, J. (1999). *Katie and the Mona Lisa.* New York: Orchard.
Mayhew, J. (1999). *Katie meets the impressionists.* New York: Orchard.
Medearis, M. (2000). *Artists and their art.* Austin, TX: Steck-Vaughn.
Waldman, N. (1999). *The starry night.* Honesdale, PA: Boyds Mill Press.
Winter, J. (1994). *Diego.* New York: Dragonfly.
Winter, J. (1998). *My name is Georgia.* New York: Silver Whistle.
Winter, J. (2002). *Frida.* New York: Arthur A. Levine.

FIG. 4.3. Biographies in third grade.

- Consolidates motivation and metacognition
- Can be taught
- Can be used in other content areas (p. 609)

One of the most valuable strategies for learners to employ before, during, and after a reading is self-questioning (Palinscar & Brown, 1984). The habit of self-questioning indicates the reader is monitoring his or her understanding, which in turn promotes comprehension. Novice readers do not use reading strategies frequently or efficiently and therefore need instruction in using them (Brown & Campione, 1977). Effective instructional approaches that scaffold a habit of questioning include K–W–L (Ogle, 1986), Directed Reading–Thinking Activities (DR–TA) (Stauffer, 1969), and graphic organizers (Alvermann & Boothby, 1986). At School in the Park, students use graphic organizers to promote self-questioning before reading. These questioning habits are reinforced by their classroom teachers through the structured questioning of K–W–L and DR–TA before, during, and after reading.

Reading the Historical World

Perception. Aida Allen's third-grade students were immersed in the history of a people who lived on the land now occupied by Balboa Park. The San Diego Historical Society served as the setting for a weeklong exploration of the lives and culture of the Kumeyaay, a band of Native Americans with a current population of 20,000 in San Diego County. The Kumeyaay were the Native Americans encountered by Father Junipero Serra in 1769 when he arrived in the area to build the first of 21 California missions.

In order to understand a life very different from their own, museum educator Sherrin Landis and Ms. Allen began by focusing on vocabulary. Because all of Ms. Allen's students were English-language learners, building vocabulary would be essential for meaningful learning. The words selected for this unit included *values, culture, arts, religion, traditions, language,* and *customs.* A large foam puzzle featuring each target word and a picture was displayed and served as a unit organizer for the entire week. As the museum educator discussed the meaning and examples of each word, the puzzle was assembled piece by piece.

Envelopes containing these vocabulary words on colorful paper shapes were distributed to students, who then walked about the room to match their shapes with those of their classmates. At each encounter, students rehearsed the meaning of their vocabulary words. The words were then used as part of the assembly of a culture box of the student's own construction. When completed, these paper boxes were covered with the vocabulary words they had learned.

Inquiry. After completing the culture boxes, the students were led to the display of photographs from San Diego history. Before they could recognize the elements of culture in Kumeyaay society, they needed to become aware of their own. Pictures of people at the movie theater, dining in restaurants, and riding in their automobiles were displayed alongside photographs of cityscapes and military equipment. Could they locate examples of culture and customs in the photographs? Using the culture boxes as a memory device, students eagerly crowded around the black-and-white images to find examples of dress, religion, arts, and food customs. The adults monitored and guided discussions with small groups of students until all were satisfied they had located examples of each concept.

Upon returning to their workspace in the museum, students reported their findings to the class and shared their observations. They added their examples to a graphic organizer similar to the one in Fig. 4.4 on examples of culture and customs. The graphic organizer served as a scaffold to self-questioning because the items in need of completion generate inquiry in the mind of the learner. This graphic organizer was revisited throughout the week of study as they acquired more information. (McREL LA.5.II.1. Makes and confirms simple predictions that will be found in the text.) Thus, the students in Ms. Allen's class were introduced to a valuable strategy for learning vocabulary and organizing concepts.

Reflection. Now that students had a deeper understanding of the vocabulary and concepts associated with the study of cultures, they were ready to explore the Kumeyaay environment. Key to this was first appre-

	Components of Culture		
Vocabulary Word	*Definition*	*Present-Day Example*	*Kumeyaay Example*
Culture			
Values			
Arts			
Religion			
Tradition			
Language			
Customs			

FIG. 4.4. Components of culture graphic organizer.

ciating the landscape of the area before the arrival of the Spanish. Students learned about native plants and natural resources used by the Kumeyaay to support their way of life. Because the Kumeyaay did not have a written language, pictographs representing native plant and animal species were introduced with each new vocabulary word. The class moved outdoors to the native plant garden located in a nearby area of Balboa Park. The class worked in pairs to map the garden on an observation sheet attached to a clipboard. (McREL LA.4.II.2. Asks and seeks answers about people and places in one's local community.) Students moved about the garden looking for yucca, agave, prickly pear, scrub brush, and California holly clump grass and recorded them on the observation sheet using a map legend. Many of the children of Mexican descent were surprised to recognize the prickly pear as a native species because they thought it grew only in Mexico.

Armed with information about the state of the natural environment before 1769, the students were ready to make predictions about the Kumeyaay way of the life. (McREL LA.4.II.1. Asks and seeks answers regarding the characteristics of various places and the people who live in those places.) Students learned that the abundance of grasses provided the Kumeyaay with the materials needed to construct high-quality baskets. Willow tree branches were used for construction of shelters and the pliable bark was used for women's clothing. As objects from the museum collection were passed around, students filled in more information about the way of life among the native people of San Diego.

Students then used these graphic organizers to formulate questions with their teacher using a K–W–L prereading strategy (Ogle, 1986). Ms. Allen later conducted several shared readings about Kumeyaay shelter, clothing, and food using a Directed Reading–Thinking Activity (DR–TA) to strengthen their use of reading strategies (Stauffer, 1969). (NBPTS RLA.IX. Reading teachers develop strategic readers.) The DR–TA mirrors the learning experiences at the Historical Society because it begins with vocabulary, then moves to a cycle of self-questioning throughout the text. Learning about the Kumeyaay continued once they had returned to Rosa Parks. Ms. Allen used *Indians of the Oaks* (Lee, 1978) as a shared reading experience, always including questions throughout the text. Students extended their knowledge by reading a number of books about Native Americans of the southwest United States and developing their own graphic organizers comparing the Kumeyaay culture with the Navaho, Pueblo, and Hopi tribes. (MN: NBPTS RLA.IX. Reading teachers create effective instruction so that readers can negotiate, inquire about, and construct meaning across the curriculum.) A list of books used by the class appears in Fig. 4.5.

Books on Native American Life

Bonvillain, N. (1994). *Hopi: Indians of North America.* Langhorne, PA: Chelsea House.
Breeden, R. L. (1979). *America's majestic canyons.* Washington, DC: National Geographic Society.
Cameron, R., & Morgan, N. (1991). *Above San Diego: A new collection of historical and original aerial photographs of San Diego.* San Diego: Author.
Clark, A. N. (1990). *Little boy with three names: Stories of Taos pueblo.* Santa Fe, NM: Ancient City.
Flanagan, M. K. (1998). *The Pueblos.* New York: Children's Press.
Lee, M. H. (1978). *Indians of the oaks.* Ramona, CA: Acoma.
Miles, M. (1985). *Annie and the old one.* New York: Little & Brown.
Moreillon, J. (1997). *Sing down the rain.* Las Cruces, NM: Kiva.
Osinski, A. (1994). *The Navajo.* New York: Children's Press.
Roessel, M. (1995). *Songs from the loom: A Navajo girl learns to weave.* Minneapolis, MN: Lerner.
Rohmer, H. (1997). *Honoring our ancestors: Stories and pictures by fourteen artists.* Watertown, MA: Charlesbridge.

FIG. 4.5. Books on Native American life.

APPLICATIONS

School in the Park is a partnership that takes advantage of several unique factors—a consortium of museums, an interested elementary school, an engaged university, and a benefactor with the vision and wherewithal to make it happen. However, the focus of this book is not on faithfully replicating this particular model but rather to spark conversations as communities large and small seek ways to take advantage of the learning resources distinctively available. Specific to this chapter is how reading instruction can be fostered by use of these distinctive resources. The following section describes possible approaches for schools and museums with limited time allowances.

What Could Be Accomplished in 5 Days?

The scenarios described previously in this chapter are lessons from weeklong units of instruction. In each case, the learning sequence was constructed to first introduce the students to an aspect of the biological, artistic, or historical world through the use of the artifacts and exhibits in the museums. The museum educator took a lead on this part of the instruction because he or she possesses the content knowledge necessary to make the most of the exhibits. Teachers collaborate with the museum staff to deliver a sequence of instruction based on sound pedagogical principles designed to foster inquiry. As I observed, the inquiry was well suited to promote reading as part of a comprehensive literacy development program. In all cases, museum and school personnel team to develop curriculum that is standards based. This commitment to academic standards makes it possible for teachers to extend the learning experiences through the days and weeks preceding and following the visit. In many cases, this is where the true reflection occurs as students identify connections with other texts, with their personal experiences, and with the larger world (Zimmerman & Keene, 1997).

What Could Be Accomplished in 3 Days?

A 3-day standards-based sequence at a museum location can offer a multitude of reading experiences. As with a 5-day visit, the time spent at the museum needs to be purposeful and focused on a particular aspect of the curriculum. This can be accomplished using an essential question to organize the learning sequence. For example, a visit to an anthropological museum can be organized around the essential question, "How and why do humans celebrate?" Student perception is established by visiting exhibits featuring wedding, birth, and sacred celebrations from around the world and across time. The classroom teacher reads quality children's literature related to the essential question, such as *I'm in Charge of Celebrations* (Baylor, 1995).

Day 2 begins with the inquiry phase of learning as student teams research celebrations in disparate cultures such as pre-Columbian Peru, colonial America, the island nations of Oceania, and Ghana before the slave traders arrived. Day 3 is the time for reflective learning as students make connections to their own communities and cultures. Working as partners, students use disposable cameras to capture images of celebrations in the museum. Once they return to school, the film can be developed to create photo essays to answer the essential question.

What Can Be Accomplished in 1 Day?

A 1-day standards-based visit to a museum can be elevated above the typical field trip experience through planning and instruction in anticipation of and subsequent to the visit. As with the longer sequences, it is advisable to first delineate the content standards that will be addressed and to identify a particular theme or essential question to organize student learning. In the days and weeks before the visit, the teacher should share narrative and informational texts related to the content of the visit. Literature circles using books containing related themes can be read to build background knowledge and spur discussion. Consider using the information available on the Internet as a method for presenting information in advance of the visit. A WebQuest is a linked sequence of websites that have been supplemented with learning objectives and projects (Dodge, 1995). Hundreds of WebQuests constructed by K to 12 teachers all over the country are available at http://www.webquest.org. For instance, a 1-day trip by middle school students to the local science museum can be preceded by a WebQuest on changes to the ozone layer over Antarctica. Students must research the effects on the penguin population and determine whether ultraviolet radiation is causing harmful changes to the biosystem. The WebQuest culminates in an international symposium on environmental changes hosted by students who present their findings. In this context, the science museum is transformed from a field trip destination to a community resource for budding researchers. Students can interview museum personnel to uncover information needed for their symposium presentation. These virtual relationships can be maintained over a long period of time especially as museum, university, and other community experts are identified.

One-day interactive learning projects like this can be hosted in virtually any museum or community destination. A trip to the library can become a key part of a class project to put banned books on trial. Young children can participate in a Zoo Bingo activity to catalog animal enclosures they visit. Nearly any museum visit can be organized around a scavenger hunt for artifacts on display in the exhibits.

CONCLUSION

I saw ample evidence and examples of how the learning environment of the museum presents an outstanding opportunity to build and extend student reading by building background knowledge. Experiences with the artifacts and exhibits of the museum work because they make students aware of the biological, artistic, and historical world beyond the classroom walls. Research-based instructional practices establish a sense of inquiry that propels student learning and allows the teacher to introduce text that becomes meaningful because the content is more familiar. Student knowledge is solidified through reflective learning and standards-based experiences that occur at the museum and in their classrooms, allowing them to draw on the information months and even years later. The comments of School in the Park graduates now attending middle school echo this last statement. One student observed, "I am more relaxed and confident because I learned things in School in the Park that I can use here [middle school]." Another offered, "Things we learned in SITP, we are learning again in middle school. So we sort of know it already."

In Greek mythology, there are no coincidences and every event is laden with meaning. It should come as no surprise then that the mother of the nine muses was Mnemosyne, the goddess of memory and inventor of words. Nine-year-old Dulce's quest for a book about muses is a perfect illustration of the power of memory, the importance of reading the world, and the resulting thirst of a self-directed learner for words that will answer her questions.

REFERENCES

Aliki. (1997). *The gods and goddesses of Olympus*. New York: HarperTrophy.

Allen, J. (2002). *On the same page: Shared reading beyond the primary grades*. York, ME: Stenhouse.

Alvermann, D. E., & Boothby, P. R. (1986). Children's transfer of graphic organizer instruction. *Reading Psychology, 7*(2), 87–100.

Armbruster, B. B., & Osborn, J. H. (2002). *Reading instruction and assessment: Understanding the IRA standards*. Newark, DE: International Reading Association.

Baylor, B. (1995). *I'm in charge of celebrations*. New York: Aladdin.

Bear, D. R., Invernizzi, M., Templeton, S., & Johnston, F. (2004). *Words their way: Word study for phonics, vocabulary, and spelling instruction* (3rd ed.). Upper Saddle River, NJ: Pearson Merrill Prentice Hall.

Brown, A. L., & Campione, J. C. (1977). *Memory strategies in learning: Training children to study strategically*. Urbana, IL: Illinois University Center for Reading.

Daniels, H. (2002). *Literature circles: Voice and choice in book clubs and reading circles* (2nd ed.). York, ME: Stenhouse.

Dodge, B. (1995). WebQuests: A technique for Internet-based learning. *Distance Educator, 1*(2), 10–13.

Fearn, L., & Farnan, N. (2001). *Interactions: Teaching writing and the language arts*. Boston: Mifflin.

Fisher, D., Flood, J., Lapp, D., & Frey, N. (2004). Interactive read-alouds: Is there a common set of implementation practices? *The Reading Teacher, 58,* 8–17.

Fisher, D., & Frey, N. (2003). Writing instruction for struggling adolescent readers: A gradual release model. *Journal of Adolescent & Literacy, 46,* 396–405.

Fountas, I. C., & Pinnell, G. S. (2001). *Guiding readers and writers grades 3–6: Teaching comprehension, genre, and content literacy*. Portsmouth, NH: Heinemann.

Freire, P., & Macedo, D. P. (1987). *Literacy: Reading the word and the world*. New York: Bergin & Garvey.

Frey, N., & Fisher, D. (2006). *The language arts workshop: Purposeful reading and writing instruction*. Upper Saddle River, NJ: Merrill Prentice Hall.

Harris, T. L., & Hodges, R. E. (Eds.). (1995). *The literacy dictionary: The vocabulary of reading and writing*. Newark, DE: International Reading Association.

Holdaway, D. (1979). *The foundations of literacy*. New York: Scholastic.

Ivey, G., & Broaddus, K. (2001). "Just plain reading": A survey of what makes students want to read in middle school classrooms. *Reading Research Quarterly, 36,* 350–377.

Juel, C., Biancarosa, G., Coker, D., & Deffes, R. (2003). Walking with Rosie: A cautionary tale of early reading instruction. *Educational Leadership, 60*(7), 12–18.

Lee, M. H. (1978). *Indian of the Oaks*. Ramona, CA: Acoma.

Mid-Continent Regional Education Laboratory. (2004). *Compendium of standards and benchmarks for K–12 education* (4th ed.). Retrieved April 1, 2004, from www.mcrel.org/compendium/kskillsIntro.asp

National Board of Professional Teaching Standards. (2002). *Early and middle childhood/literacy: Reading-language arts standards.* Detroit, MI: Author.

Ogle, D. M. (1986). K–W–L: A teaching model that develops active reading of expository text. *The Reading Teacher, 39,* 564–570.

Palincsar, A. S., & Brown, A. L. (1984). Reciprocal teaching of comprehension-monitoring activities. *Cognition and Instruction, 1,* 117–175.

Paris, S. G., Wasik, B. A., & Turner, J. C. (1991). The development of strategic readers. In R. Barr, M. L. Kamil, P. Mosenthal, & P. D. Pearson (Eds.), *Handbook of reading research* (Vol. II, pp. 609–640). Mahwah, NJ: Lawrence Erlbaum Associates.

Pearson, P. D., & Fielding, L. (1991). Comprehension instruction. In R. Barr, M. L. Kamil, P. Mosenthal, & P. D. Pearson (Eds.), *Handbook of reading research* (Vol. II, pp. 815–860). Mahwah, NJ: Lawrence Erlbaum Associates.

Pilgreen, J. (2000). *The SSR handbook: How to organize and manage a sustained silent reading program.* Portsmouth, NH: Heinemann.

Rosenblatt, L. M. (1978). *The reader, the text, the poem: The transactional theory of the literary work.* Carbondale, IL: Southern Illinois University Press.

Rosenblatt, L. M. (2003). Literary theory. In J. Flood, D. Lapp, J. R. Squire, & J. M. Jensen (Eds.), *Handbook of research on teaching the English language arts* (2nd ed., pp. 67–73). Mahwah, NJ: Lawrence Erlbaum Associates.

Samuels, J., & Kamil, M. L. (1984). Models of the reading process. In P. D. Pearson, R. Barr, M. L. Kamil, & P. Mosenthal (Eds.), *Handbook of reading research* (pp. 185–224). Mahwah, NJ: Lawrence Erlbaum Associates.

Snow, C. E., Burns, M. S., & Griffin, P. (Eds.). (1998). *Preventing reading difficulties in young children.* Washington, DC: National Academy Press.

Spencer, S. (2002). *School in the park: Making connections. Third year report 2001–2002.* San Diego, CA: City Heights Educational Collaborative.

Stanovich, K. E. (1986). Matthew effects in reading: Some consequences of individual differences in the acquisition of literacy. *Reading Research Quarterly,* 360–407.

Stauffer, R. G. (1969). *Directing reading maturity as a cognitive process.* New York: Harper & Row.

Sticht, T. (1988–1989). Adult literacy education. In E. Rothkopf (Ed.), *Review of research in education* (pp. 59–96). Washington, DC: American Education Research Association.

Zimmerman, S., & Keene, E. O. (1997). *Mosaic of thought: Teaching comprehension in a reader's workshop.* Portsmouth, NH: Heinemann.

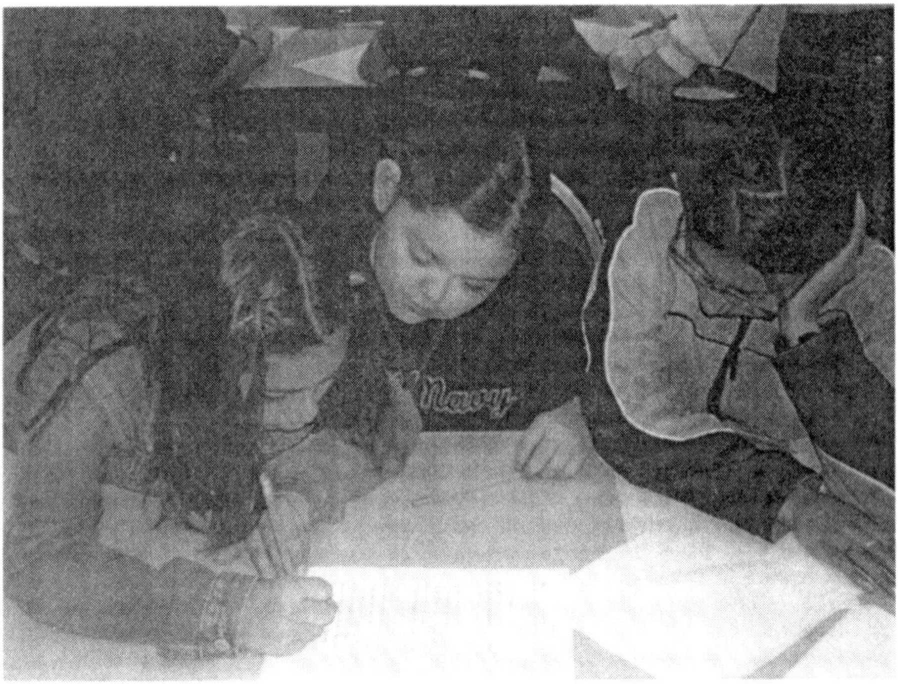
Navy

CHAPTER FIVE

An Authentic Context for Writing to Learn and Teaching Writing Intentionally

Leif Fearn
Nancy Farnan

We have written a great deal about writing and writing instruction and were quite excited to be asked to critique the impact and opportunities School in the Park presents for young and emerging writers.

June 26. Four fifth-grade boys commit deliberate attention to several photographs, with *deliberate attention* meaning focused concentration, not merely *good* behavior. They are working in the San Diego Historical Society's *special library*, the archives of primary sources. They are looking at diaries, maps, and photographs at various stations that have been set up in this archival room. The docent reviewed the concept of *archive* and included the words, with explanation, *exposition, exhibit,* and *rotation,* all because Balboa Park, the site of the centers of learning for School in the Park, began as the site of the Pan American Exposition. During the docent's explanations and directions, she used and contextualized nine more words and phrases: *newer, older, definitely, observation, noticing, versus, change, based on the evidence,* and *chronological order.* There are scores of photographs of the 20th century's middle years. The learning focus for the session is early leaders in San Diego. In addition to the photographs, the display includes architectural drawings and maps of the park and surrounding area.

Students do investigations at each station. The four boys handle several photographs, looking very closely and drawing conclusions from details. They had been directed to look for nuances in the photos on the basis of which they could make inferences about which is newer and which is older. The cues included architectural features, the existence of automobiles, the appearance of automobiles, horses and carriages, and stages of development in the park.

They studied and talked with one another about the photographs and what they observed. They arranged the several photographs in chronological order. Then they discovered that there were dates on the back of each photograph. The dates confirmed their order, save for two, which had been reversed. They looked again at those photographs and realized that they'd missed one detail on a building. They were proud of their work.

That was a small vignette, perhaps a minor one to a casual observer, especially someone unfamiliar with schools. To a school person, however, the vignette is dramatic. One, the boys were not just talking, as fifth graders do; they were talking about content and some complex processes associated with the management, organization, and understanding of content. It was not merely catching and remembering facts in social studies; it was observing and reasoning about social studies content. And the social studies included architecture, photography, and transportation systems (Curriculum and Instruction Steering Committee of National Center for History in the Schools, 1994).

Maybe it wasn't social studies. Maybe it was the arts. It's hard to make subject matter distinctions in the midst of learning. Subject matter distinctions are largely about teaching. Much of what characterizes School in the Park is the emphasis on learning.

That, in itself, is noteworthy, but the vignette was dramatic for two other reasons that lie at the heart of this chapter. One has to do with a paradigm change three decades ago in writing instruction. There was a change of focus from product to process (Emig, 1971; Fearn & Farnan, 2001). Young writers up to the last third of the 20th century, and for virtually all the years before, focused their attention on *what* they wrote because their teachers focused their instruction on assigning writing for young writers to produce. Then between 1965 and 1975 the focus changed to *how* young writers approached and performed a writing task. Thus the *process* approach to teaching writing began. Teachers talked of a writing curriculum they called *process* writing, and their classrooms were festooned with charts about *the* writing process.

Second, the vignette highlights the central characteristic of School in the Park, that is, taking learning outside classroom walls to integrate it into real-world, or some might say *authentic*, experiences. The focus of this chapter is on the writing experiences of students who attended School in the Park. However, it is important to keep in mind that those experiences occurred in the context of content and curriculum as they existed in real-world environments—outside the context of rows of desks and school buildings.

WRITING AND WRITING INSTRUCTION

There are over 30 years' worth of national, state, and district writing sample data available now. The data reveal two primary flaws in the assumption on which the *process* approach rests. Young writers write more today than ever before, but not appreciably better (Perksy, Daane, & Jin, 2002), which reveals the flawed assumption that they'll write better if they write more. The other flawed assumption is that practice makes perfect. It does not. Practice makes permanent; only perfect practice makes perfect, and perfect practice rests on intentional writing instruction (Fearn & Farnan, 2001).

According to the National Commission on Writing in America's Schools and Colleges (2003), "Writing, education's second *R*, has become the neglected element of American school reform" (p. 9). The Commission's report continues:

> Despite the neglect of writing instruction, it would be false to claim that most students cannot write. What most students cannot do is write well. At least, they cannot write well enough to meet the demands they face in higher education and the emerging work environment. Basic writing is not the issue; the problem is that most students cannot write with the skill expected of them today. (p. 16)

The Commission urged that time must be committed for writing instruction, and critical to a time commitment is instruction that makes a measurable difference in students' writing effectiveness.

Intentional writing instruction, defined as purposeful and explicit teaching "on the systems for how writing works, the various formats, procedural knowledge, and conventions" (Fearn & Farnan, 2001, p. 37), is this chapter's focus, and School in the Park is the context. Consider the context for intentional writing instruction represented by those boys' conversation that morning as they pored over 80-year-old photographs in an effort to make chronological distinctions among them.

To write well, young writers, or any writers, for that matter, must have something to think and write about. Writing, more than anything else, is thinking. People write to make sense of what they know and care about. They use language to explore and record their sense-making and to communicate their thinking and the sense they make. In school, young writers are supposed to make sense of school curriculum, and they're supposed to care about the sense they make. Then they're supposed to record and communicate the sense-making and the end result of that process.

The most effective students in school are the ones who figure out what the subject matter is and how it works, alone and in interactions with other subject matter. That is most likely to occur if students are actively engaged in making sense in as authentic a manner as possible. When adults teach students a version of sense already made by others, students often are not engaged. They need the tools, the background, to engage. Many students don't have that background. They are not poor students, and they are not disadvantaged. They're simply not engaged; perhaps they're even bored because there is nothing for them to do. The four boys in our vignette had something to do.

In school, students are supposed to write about the meanings they've constructed in social studies, science, the aesthetics, literature, mathematics, and so forth. To the extent that students have not done the constructing from school curriculum, or made the language of school curriculum their own, they have little to write about in school.

The four fifth-grade boys were observing and making inferences about chronological order from primary documents in history, and they were using the language of observation and history to do so. They were engaged, they were making sense of history, and they had something to write about.

Now to writing itself. Most of the young writers in school today write so much more than any of their agemates in previous years, though no better. They get lots of writing practice, but little, if any, intentional writing instruction that prescribes how to go about the writing. They receive years' worth of descriptions about what's in a sentence once it has been written (subject, predicate, modification, *complete* thought, and so forth), but no prescriptions about how to write one. School in the Park students, both at the park and on their school site, received daily intentional instruction that focused on how to write sentences, interactions between and among sentences, interactions between and among paragraphs, meaning-markers, and the genres.

More specifically, teachers who teach writing intentionally and well know enough to teach according to their answers to the following basic questions.

1. You are designing a lesson sequence about thinking and writing in sentences for (pick a grade). You may not refer to the "completeness" of thoughts, subjects and predicates, nouns and verbs, big letters and dots, or numbers of words. How will you frame the first three lessons?
2. You are designing a lesson sequence about capitalization and punctuation for (pick a grade). You may not refer to rule statements, and you may not use any form of editing sheet. How will you frame the first three lessons?
3. You are planning a lesson sequence about paragraph thinking and writing for (pick a grade). You may not refer to numbers of sen-

tences, kinds of sentences, fast food metaphors, geometric shapes, or architectural designs. How will you frame the first three lessons?
4. You are planning a lesson sequence about descriptive writing, and you may not refer to kinds or definitions of words, nor to any part of "speech." How will you frame at least two lessons?
5. You are planning a lesson sequence about (pick a genre) for (pick a grade). You may not refer to any physical design of any sort—no formula, no numbers of sentences or paragraphs, no geometric shapes. How will you frame the first three lessons?

People who understand writing and writing instruction are known by their responses to those kinds of questions. In each instance, we have removed the crutches, the *teacherisms*, and we have left the teacher-planner with what writing is and, therefore, what we should be teaching young writers about writing. School in the Park teachers are prepared to think, plan, and teach on the basis of answers to those kinds of questions.

But no matter how much instruction students receive, if they have little or nothing to write about because they have little or nothing they have constructed, they will still not learn to write well. Young writers need instruction about *how* to write as well as the opportunity to construct meanings they can care about because they know something; they have experienced the focused concentration necessary for learning. That is what School in the Park did for those four boys on that June morning.

Writing To Learn

Most readers of this page have had the experience of reading and suddenly realizing that they do not have the remotest idea of what they have been reading because they were not paying attention. When that happens, we go back to where we think we checked out; and we begin again, recognizing mileposts along the way because we were there just moments ago, and pieces were automatically registered in active memory. But the second read is what helps us make meaning. The first was eye movements and periodic fixations on words and phrases, but no comprehension, no construction of meaning. People can read that way, and young readers read that way a lot and need to be taught what attention means during the reading act. That is the reason for shared and guided reading, for think-alouds and reflection.

But no one ever writes that way. Readers of this page have never sat at the keyboard, constructing text, only to realize at the bottom of a page or at the end of a paragraph that there is text but little or no awareness of what it means or how it got there because we were not paying attention.

People cannot write while paying attention to something else. That is an enormous advantage for teachers because it is through learners' attention that learning occurs. Students *can*, and they often do, learn from their reading; but they *will*, and they always will, learn from their writing.

When learners write, they describe and explain, and much of what they have to learn in school is descriptive and explanatory. They make connections, and much of the knowledge they construct is the connective tissue, the relationships, they form between and among experiences with school content. Writing is capturing, defining, and recording. School in the Park offers compelling things to define and describe, to capture, to record. It is also a place where the content of school comes alive and engages learners who can construct the connections that become knowledge.

Nineteen third graders wrote in their travel journals about the Silk Road. They had just come from a museum where a docent guided them through silken eras. They were in the West Wing of the Museum of Modern Art and walked into a gallery (a word the museum educator used) where Chinese artifacts (another of her words) were located. The museum educator walked with students to a Chinese rug on the wall, originally used in a palace. She prompts, "Remember when we were in Italy during the Renaissance?" The discussion centers on gold spun into the carpet and the symbols there: a vibrant dragon comprised of bright red, green, yellow, and gold in the center of the rug, a symbol for protection and strength. "Remember, a symbol is something like a picture that stands for something else, an idea or concept." A student asks, "Why is the dragon this symbol?" To which the museum educator replied, "That's a very good research question for us. Let's not forget about it."

Students observed and asked questions about tapestries too large to hang in even large homes, robes of gold and scarlet, and a display of the worm that makes the silk from which the wall hangings and robes were woven. They saw the maps, pictures of the camels and their footprints in the sand, the mountain passes, the architecture of the cities, the peoples along the way. Students toured the museum and then convened in a bright room with round tables and student-sized chairs, a felt map of the silk road covering one wall, and blue and green painted cubicles lined with books across the back wall. The museum educator was a river of oral language, all contextualized by images of landmarks, cultures, and history.

The children's writing was in response to Power Writing, one of five short cues (Fearn & Farnan, 2001), this one designed to promote students' writing fluency and provide them with an opportunity to record their thinking about what they were learning. In Round 1, each young writer selected between the ideas of *journey* and *rice* and were directed to write as much as they could, as well as they could, in 60 seconds. Every child wrote for all of the 60 seconds, and every child read what he or she wrote to a partner. Then, there was Round 2 (*silk* and *buy*), writing for 60 seconds followed again by reading to a partner. After three rounds, the museum educator asked students to choose their favorite writing and solicited volunteers to share what they wrote.

A student wrote: "I'm Bianca, and I'm going to Baghdad. I'm going to trade gold for horses. I'm going to bring gold so it can be traded for horses. I'm from Byzantium. I'm nine years old. I have brown hair. I'm going to bring a lot of water, fruit, clothes, and food for me and for the camel."

Notice that Jorge has the concepts: "I'm traveling from Chang'an to Byzantium. I'm traveling because I want to get things from different places. I want to trade silk for other things."

It took the third graders 6 minutes to draft three writings, read aloud in dyads, and share with the larger group.

The museum educator continues, "You are now in AD 800, in Kashgar—on what continent?"

Students reply in chorus, "Asia."

The museum educator asks, "In what country?"

Again the chorus, "China."

"You are merchants. On our journey on our camels, we all took one thing to barter and sell. What was that thing?"

One student replies, "Silk."

The museum educator comments that their "trip" from Chang'an to Kashgar on camels was very trying. She asks them to write for 5 minutes about this part of the trip. Students turn immediately to their journals to record that experience. After 5 minutes, she asks them to share what they wrote. Students describe not sleeping very well because the desert is cold at night. They discuss their experiences crossing the desert, the daytime travel through the Land of No Return. They describe seeing a cobra, a rattlesnake.

One student writes (unedited):

I'm starting my journey. I feel worried, because what if something goes wrong. When we go to the dessert I will put on my long pants. I will pack vegetables, a notebook to write how I feel. I will pack water, clothes, and my passport for any case. I named my camel Honey because the color of her skin looks like honey, and because my camel is a female. I brought my dad and my friend. My mom is in heaven hoping we have a good, careful trip.

Another young writer writes (unedited):

I feel excited, but scared because I'm going on a trip throuw the desert. When I'm going in the desert that's more than 200 miles, I need a whole lot of water. I'm going to pack 30 gallons of water, and blankets made out of silk. On my way, I could also bring something to entertain me. Of course I would bring my passport. I could even barder. Since I'm going throuw the worst desert, I could bring 3 camels. I'm scared something might go wrong, and I could end up as bones on the dunes. I would also need water and food for my camel. My camels are all serious.

After listening to a few student writings, the museum educator went to the felt map and asked students how many miles they have traveled from Chang'an to Kashgar. The map is designed with a grid of squares in the background. Each square represents 100 miles, so students calculate how far they've come. They conclude that they've come 2,200 miles on this leg of their journey, which eventually will take them to Byzantium. Wanting student to anticipate what is ahead of them, she tells students that after spending the night in Kashgar, they will be on the road to Baghdad tomorrow. "How far to Baghdad? Raise your hand when you figure it out." Some students take pencils in hand to do calculations. Others study the map, doing mental calculations.

In just under a minute, students' raised hands interrupt the working silence. "2,200 miles," one student calls out, "same as from Chang'an to Kashgar."

The next question is, "So how far have we come altogether?"

It's only a moment before several hands go up, and a student reports, "4,400 miles."

The museum educator puts legend icons on the map to symbolize the desert and oasis. On their own maps at their tables, students create legend boxes at the bottom of their maps, put those legends on the map in the appropriate places, and color up to where they are on their route. Finally, they write once again in their Passport Logs. The teacher prompts, "Write about some of the things you see in Kashgar. Food? What you might trade for? Who you might meet there?"

So Much to Talk and Write About. At this point, the School in the Park teacher took over. "Why was it called the 'Silk' Road?" There was a lot of talk that became progressively better informed during the 2-minute discussion. "What's the difference between trading and buying with money?" Again, there were just under 2 minutes of teacher-led conversation that became increasingly informed.

"What do you know?" she asked. The children volunteered *silk worms, water immersion, trading goods, camels* and *boats, Italy* and *China, Sanskrit, Hundu, India.*

A third grader called out, "Namaste," *good morning* in India.

The teacher points to some pictures on the wall. "What words would you use to describe the architecture of Kashgar? What is architecture?"

A student replies, "The design of buildings." They note that the architecture of Kashgar looks like rectangles. The teacher points out that the buildings here look different from those in Chang'an. She comments that China is a very large country and that as they journey across it, they have seen cultural changes, some of which are found in the architecture.

Students see a picture of *ruins*. They discuss that Kashgar is a place with water, an *oasis*, one of the words on a word wall, and talk about the fact that Kashgar grew to be a large city in the middle of the desert because of the water source. The discussion continues about the market and the fact that merchants who traveled the Silk Road came from all over to the market. One student comments that "people buy, barter, trade, sell, and do business. It's like a fair, people of all cultures come to Kashgar." There are frequent references to the wall map and the idea that cultures change across the miles. One student makes a reference to California and comments that he knows people from lots of different cultures. Throughout these conversations, it would be difficult to miss students' engagement, their enthusiasm for their *journey* as part of a *caravan*, and the rich vocabulary they were using to describe their experiences. It would be difficult to miss the fact that students are making sense, learning the words to capture their understandings, and building a store of knowledge necessary for informed conversation and writing.

On another day, four adults are in the room with 19 third graders. Students calculate the mileage from Baghdad to Tyre (600 miles) and how far they have come since leaving Chang'an (5,500 miles). The teacher explains that Tyre (pronounced like *tire*) is on the Mediterranean Sea, that it's a harbor. She holds up a large picture of San Diego Bay and says that Tyre, like San Diego, is a city on a harbor, a port city. The adults help students arrange their chairs facing a blank wall, and a slide projector illuminates an image of a caravan leaving Baghdad on its way to Tyre. The museum educator notes that the camel prints get smaller in the distance and that camels' feet do not sink far into the sand because their hooves are broad and are made for walking on sand. Another museum educator standing at the projector asks students to look at the landscape and notice the mountains, valley, and desert—the varied terrain. He notes that "It's rocky. The river is at the bottom of the valley; it's called the valley floor. Why do you think the river is at the bottom of the valley?"

A student responds, "The water goes to the bottom of the valley out of the mountains."

The museum educator continues, "Here is the country called Italy; the city is Florence. Which is the country and which is the city, like China and Chang'an."

There is a slide of the coastline and Mediterranean Sea. "The sea makes Tyre a port city." The next slide is of a modern-day market on the sea.

"Luis, what did you find in the market in Tyre? What kind of food would you find?"

"Fish. Seafood."

The museum educator agrees, "Yes, and how is this different from Kashgar?"

A student raises her hand: "Kashgar is in the desert. It's a different culture. It's a desert. There's an oasis. People live in different ways."

The teacher remarks that now that they are at the sea, they will no longer need their camels. In fact, they will need to sell their camels to buy boats to travel across the sea to Byzantium. She asks, "Will we paddle our boats?"

A student volunteers an enthusiastic "no. It would be too slow; we'd need to sail."

The museum educator shows a slide of boats, and the classroom teacher says, "Let's look for a boat with a sail." At this point, it occurs to a couple of students that they will have to sell their camels.

One student asks, "What will happen to my camel? I don't want to leave him." The teacher says that there is no choice. The only way to get across the water is by boat, and the only way to buy a boat is to sell the camel. There's an outcry in the room, and chorus of "No." How real has this journey become to students? They cannot conceive of leaving behind the camels that have *traveled* with them, that they have named, that have been part of their writings and conversations for several weeks.

There was an intensity in the room. Every child was engaged, only partly, maybe only marginally, because the adult–student ratio was 1 to 5. Mostly the engagement came from the enthusiasm of the teachers, the background of the students, the thrill of constructing images and ideas, and their immersion in a learning environment that brought an experience of authenticity to their learning.

When we talked with the children after the session, their talk was proud and insightful. It was about hundreds of years ago, thousands of miles away, and light years removed from any cultural frame of reference within their line of sight. They were constructing knowledge from their own experiences and under the urging of their teachers. Along the way they used the language of conceptualization—their own talk and their own writing, both shared with their peers who were also constructing the huge concepts that accommodate history, geography, economics, and cultural literacy, all in interactive patterns.

Those kinds of interactive patterns permeate most standards-based curricular frames of reference. In California, for example, sixth-grade social studies features the interactive curricular perspective, as indicated in this standard statement: "Students analyze the geographic, political, economic, religious, and social structures of the Ancient Hebrews" (California County Superintendent Educational Services Association, 2001, p. 186).

Rosa Parks students, having studied the Silk Road, will have the prior knowledge on which the tracing-of-explorers'-routes standard rests:

> Students trace the routes of early explorers and describe the early explorations of the Americas, to include biography (Christopher Columbus and Francisco Vasquez de Coronado), geography (Spain, France, England, Portugal, the Netherlands, Sweden, Russia, Africa, and West Indies), technology (gun powder, ships-building, compass, chronometer, sextant), and social/religious movements (Inquisition and Reformation) (California County Superintendent Educational Services Association, 2001, p. 132).

National standards for world history, "Intensified Hemispheric Interactions (1000–1500)," rest on the proposition that the modern world's complexities emerged as a result of maturing long-distance trade and the economic and social institutions connected to and developed by it (Curriculum and Instruction Steering Committee of National Center for History in the Schools, 1994, p. 129). Understanding this complex proposition requires the concept of interregional communication and trade. The Silk Road study at School in the Park is fundamental to standards in world history.

It is also fundamental to literacy standards, specifically in writing. At every K to 6 level (California is characteristic), writing standards refer to the sentence, simple at first, then compound and complex sentences (California Department of Education, 1999). The writing standards for sentencing, paragraphing, spelling, capitalization, punctuation, and word selection are all associated with making, recording, and communicating meaning. Moreover, the separate elements included in the writing standards have the basic utility of enhancing learning itself. That is what those third graders in the Silk Road study were doing. They were using writing—the sentencing, paragraphing, word knowledge and selection, and the mechanical devices that make writing work—as tools for learning in the social studies. If standards-based curriculum means anything at all, it means curricular studies that use developing literacy skills to accomplish large, subject-matter objectives.

Basic Literacy Practices

There are a variety of reasons why young writers don't write as well as their teachers would like. Two of the most important are that they don't know how, and they have little that is sufficiently compelling about which to write. School in the Park students have teachers on their school site who have committed themselves to teaching writing intentionally and continuously so their young writers know how. Semiannual writing sample data on students who experienced School in the Park show that the children have and can use the writing skills critical for writing well.

What the Data Show. A survey of practicing writers and an analysis of one of the seminal books about writing assessment (Spandel & Stiggins, 1997) produced a framework for writing sample assessment (Fearn & Farnan, 2001, pp. 326–329). That framework features seven attributes on which writing samples from School in the Park students were scored.

1. Clear, precise, and mature sentences
2. Recognizable organizational pattern
3. Mechanical control
4. Word selection
5. Appropriate form for the purpose
6. Writer's voice, passions, perspectives
7. Fluency

We used two assessment protocols to accommodate the seven attributes. The *analytic* protocol scored for fluency, maturity, and mechanical control. Fluency, a creative thinking skill that measures quantity (Fearn, 1976), is an artifact of word count. Given that all young writers in the analysis wrote for precisely 5 minutes, the more fluent writers received a higher score.

Maturity is an artifact of two ratios: (a) between number of words and number of sentences and (b) between number of sentences and number of clause structures. Given that maturity in writing occurs at the sentence level, more mature writers tend toward the capacity for longer and/or more complex sentences.

Mechanical control is a ratio of mechanical errors (i.e., errors in conventions) to sentences. The scorer tallies capitalization, punctuation, spelling, and sentence structure errors and divides that total by the number of sentences. A 1.0, therefore, means that the writer committed an average of one error per sentence in a writing sample.

All writing samples in the School in the Park assessment were also scored according to a *general impression* protocol (G-score) in order to accommodate attributes such as organization, elaboration, texture, focus, word selection, voice, and passion. The G-score reflects practicing writers' main priority—that a piece of writing *works*. Writing works for a variety of interacting reasons, most of which are included in the general impression scoring protocol. It is important to note that the G-score procedure rested on a 6-point *absolute* scale. That means that a score of 6 reflects a piece of writing that is as good as it can be written, not for a fifth or third grader, but for the very best writer writing as well as he or she is able. The result of that scoring procedure was average G-scores of 1.5 to 2.5 with few 3s, still fewer 4s, and two 6s among the 900 writing samples submitted by School in the Park students in the third, fourth, and fifth grades. The G-score is a measure of the kind of writing that writers refer to as *working*. It's writing that is textured, writing that leaves a print on the reader's mind or soul.

Data Charts. At the beginning of the 2001–2002 school year, the fluency, maturity, complexity, and mechanical control performance of School in the Park students and other (i.e., control) students from demographically similar schools not participating in School in the Park were not significantly different. The one significant difference between School in the Park and other students was that School in the Park students had significantly lower G-scores prior to beginning the SITP. However, in the postscoring process, School in the Park students significantly exceeded control students in both mechanical control and G-score. By itself, that means School in the Park students, at every grade level, wrote better than did the other students. By *better* is meant that School in the Park students' writing, under conditions of a time limit and specified prompt, wrote more disciplined writing; and they wrote prose that showed greater organization, elaboration, and texture.

Those data are the more impressive when fluency data are included. Although the difference between the two groups of students' fluency was not statistically significant, School in the Park students nevertheless wrote more at the end of the year than at the beginning, by an average of six words in the third grade, three in the fourth, and eight in the fifth; and at the same time they reduced their average error rate by .75 errors per sentence in the fifth grade in a 5-minute prompted sample with no time for editing and reflection. This is noteworthy because the achievement of mechanical automaticity is fundamental to writing well.

Mechanical control, whether automatic or deliberate, does not, by itself, constitute well-written prose. Writing can be flat, predictable, and disorganized, and simultaneously mechanically exact. Good writing honors readers. Form and function interact, there is discernible focus, and the writing shows readers the writer's images. We find such writing through general impression scoring that focuses on what writers recognize as writing that works. The G-score focuses on writing that works, and the data show that School in the Park students learn to write increasingly well.

That the writing performance of School in the Park students reflects both native English speakers and English learners is especially important.

The intentional instruction featured in the School in the Park writing program was used with native English speakers as well as with English language learners, and *the data show that the language young writers bring to the classroom need not influence how we teach them to write.*

A Foundation in Writing Curriculum

The previous paragraph refers to *intentional instruction* in the beginning of the second sentence and the nature of writing instruction in the latter part of it. Intentional instruction signifies a commitment to consistent and protracted time during which the writing curriculum is delivered purposefully and systematically. Writing instruction should represent the curricular nature of writing—content and processes: craft, genres, and both teaching and learning processes. Every School in the Park teacher participated in explicit staff development to prepare them to deliver intentional instruction focused on a comprehensive writing curriculum. However, School in the Park teachers were, in no *observable* way, better teachers than were teachers of the other students. The difference between the two groups of teachers was that School in the Park teachers more consistently taught writing curriculum, whereas teachers of the other students committed the same amount of time to promoting, encouraging, and causing writing. The difference in student writing performance under those two conditions is dramatic.

But what about the second reason why young writers often do not write as well as they are able, that is, the first being that they are not taught explicitly how, and the second that they have little that is sufficiently compelling about which to write?

Critical Literacy Interactions

In the midst of the Silk Road study, third-grade David wrote in his travel journal:

> I am going to Byzantium to trade for silk. I will trade with camels and food. I came here from Chang'an. On the way I saw mountains, houses, and new people. It was a learning trip.
>
> Then I stopped at Kashgar where there was a different language from mine. It was called Arabic.
>
> In Baghdad there was another language. And there was meditation by the people. I traded a horse and food for silk.

That's not too sophisticated, perhaps, but David is a third grader who wrote the three paragraphs precisely as they appear here. We observed the text over his shoulder as he drafted it. The paragraphs work because each has a main idea distinct from the other two. There is an explicit transition from each paragraph to the next that creates a sense of coherence through the larger piece. He maintains tense throughout. He got the trade business right, for he had things to exchange for what he wanted. The piece is mechanically disciplined. But most of all, it is authentic writing because it's about something.

Critical to any literacy instruction is an *interaction* between skill development and purpose. Were the skills wanting, it would not matter that David had something to communicate. Had he been at the piano with a desire to make the music playing in his ear, he could not make the music on the keyboard if he did not know which keys to strike in what patterns. That he had a story to tell about his vicarious travels along the Silk Road would matter little if he did not know how to get that story onto paper in a manner that an audience could read. Having something to tell and the skill to say it to an audience is a fundamental interaction in literacy instruction. A basic literacy practice is to ensure that young writers experience the interaction directly.

Another basic literacy practice is the oral foundation for all literacy instruction. Fifth graders are at the Reuben H. Fleet Science Center. The focus for the session is the composition of substances. It's the science of chromatography—separating mixtures into distinct parts. Groups of children use coffee filters to find colors in various inks. There is a lot of talk in each group, much of it in Spanish. The words include *density, buoyancy, occupied, volcanic, grams, measure, length*, and *liquid*. The science teacher is talking continuously, offering contexts for understanding what words mean, directing the children's use of apparatus and materials, and listening to their reports of what they are seeing and helping them frame those reports in science language.

Then the teacher directs them to computer terminals where they pursue oral and written analyses of water. The science teacher directs them to three questions: (a) Why does water get us wet? (b) What is one substance that can appear as all forms of water, and what is its name in each of three states? (c) What are the freezing and boiling points of water? Now there is more terminology: *atom, molecule, surface tension, bending light, hydrogen, oxygen, refraction*, and *transparent*. The teacher does not shy from the terminology; he merely contextualizes it when it comes up in his *patter*, his oral language.

The children wrote what they found. Two boys wrote, "When you look at a pencil dipped in water, it looks like the pencil is crooked, but it's just refraction."

Two other children wrote, "It's interesting that water can look like it's too high for the glass to hold, but it doesn't spill."

Language is learned in the ear. Writing's foundation is oral, not visual or tactile. A basic practice in writing instruction is teacher talk, both to contextualize student writing and to repeat student read-alouds of their writing. Young writers have to know what accomplished writers know—what language sounds like when it is written down. The science teacher used the language of science consistently, even relentlessly, as *instructional patter*. When we read the children's sentences, they contained the science terminology and context they heard in the teacher's patter, but in their own words.

HOW DO WE USE COMMUNITY RESOURCES FOR WRITING INSTRUCTION?

Make no mistake. The young writers whom we described in this chapter were very enthusiastic about their hours at the park, but that is not where they learned to write increasingly well as the data showed. They learned to write through instruction that centered on a comprehensive writing curriculum. School in the Park provided a compelling context and interesting ideas and images, including a rich vocabulary to support their learning and with which to communicate. School in the Park explicitly reinforced teachers' intentional writing instruction—in a seemingly nonschool context. All of that is very important.

But it is also important that students are able to write when they have something interesting and compelling to write about. If we take students into the community for authentic experiences designed to broaden their contexts and they have no tools with which to record and communicate, it's only a field trip.

One critical element of writing in the park is the intentional instruction that supports it, both at the school site and in the park. The museum educators were exemplary educators. Their Rosa Parks teaching partners were also expert at what they did. Together, the instructional experience was greater than it could have been at the neighborhood school or at the park under the direction of one group of teachers or the other. School in the Park's influence on writing is an artifact of extraordinary teachers.

Also, no one should risk ignoring the importance of reinforcing intentional writing instruction *in a seemingly nonschool context*. For as long as writing instruction and writing behavior occur in school, alone, writing will forever be a school activity, utterly removed from its fundamental purposes—the writer's need to record and communicate. Mark Twain wrote that it makes no difference whether a man can or cannot read, if he doesn't. In precisely the same way, it makes no difference whether or not a person can write if he or she does not use writing to satisfy the human need to record and communicate.

And finally, students' enthusiasm for writing and their documented writing performance was common with the participating third, fourth, and fifth graders. Of course, the opportunity to spend their school days surrounded by the wonders of San Diego's magnificent Balboa Park would compel any 8-, 9-, and 10-year-old. But these 8-, 9-, and 10-year-olds were studying at this park, not just visiting. The novelty of the bus trip wears off very fast. Then the reality of daily learning logs, writing and sharing, fluency, mechanical discipline, deliberate attention, and behavioral responsibility kick in. The boys and girls in this program stayed the course. Their enthusiasm did not wear thin, and there is a reason no reader of this chapter should fail to recognize. These children were learning every day. More than half of them spoke a native language other than English, and all of the experiences were in English. Every one of them wrote in English about things often hundreds of years ago in places often thousands of miles away. They held their focus because they were learning. Learning is the predominant reinforcer. Learning is the foundation of School in the Park.

REFERENCES

California County Superintendent Educational Services Association. (2001). *Pages of the past: Literature aligned to California history–social science standards, grades K–6*. Sacramento, CA: Author.

California Department of Education. (1999). *Reading/language arts framework for California public schools: Kindergarten through grade twelve*. Sacramento, CA: Author.

Curriculum and Instruction Steering Committee of National Center for History in the Schools. (1994). *National standards for world history: Exploring paths to the present*. University of California, Los Angeles: Author.

Emig, J. (1971). *The composing processes of twelfth graders*. Urbana, IL: National Council of Teachers of English.

Fearn, L. (1976). Individual development: A process model in creativity. *Journal of Creative Behavior, 10*, 55–64.

Fearn, L., & Farnan, N. (2001). *Interactions: Teaching writing and the language arts*. Boston, MA: Houghton Mifflin.

National Commission on Writing in America's Schools and Colleges. (2003). *The neglected 'R': The need for a writing revolution*. College Entrance Examination Board.

Perksy, H., Daane, M., & Jin, Y. (2002). *The nation's report card: Writing 2002*. National Center for Education Statistics. Retrieved May 14, 2005, from http://nces.ed.gov/pubsearch/pubsinfo.asp?pubid=2003529

Spandel, V., & Stiggins, R. J. (1997). *Creating writers: Linking assessment to instruction* (2nd ed.). New York: Longman.

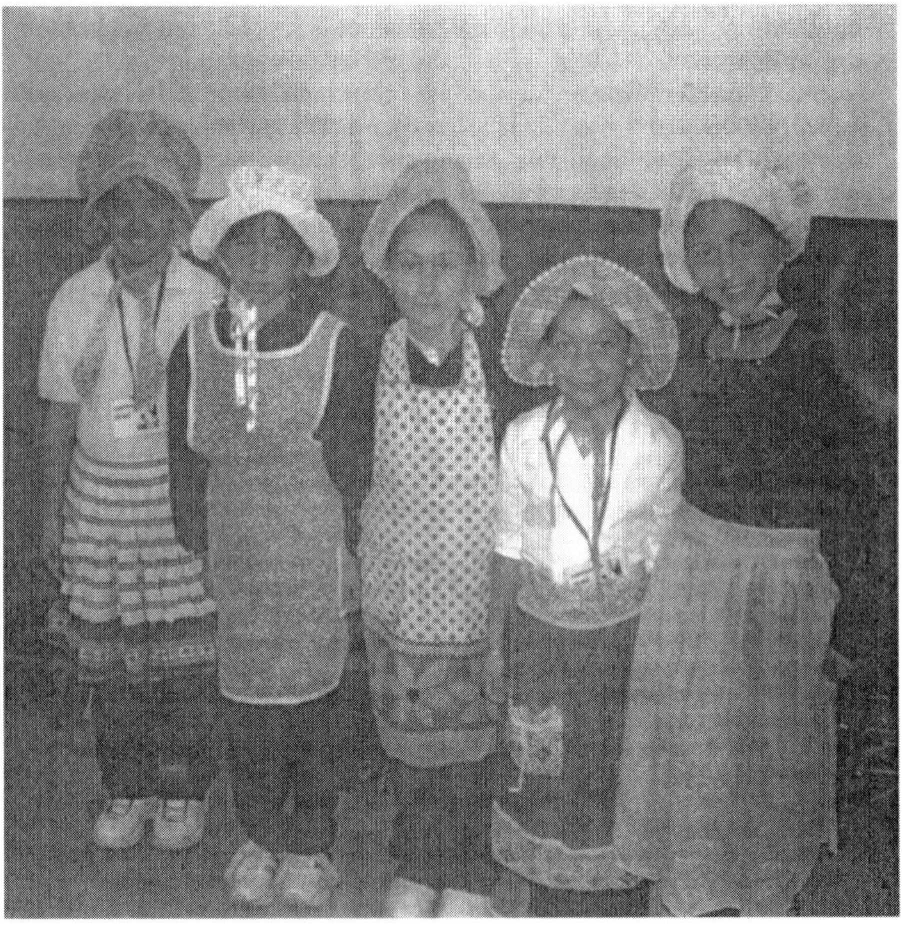

CHAPTER SIX

Arts as a Centerpiece for Integrated Learning

Nan L. McDonald

PRELUDE

There's a new culture here in School in the Park. We've made the conscious decision to teach the whole child. We put the child back in childhood. Here we learn with experimentation, wonder, discovery—by finding out, looking, and using the child's creative imagination. All of this has been somewhat lost in our society and in this generation. If we really want to change their lives, they've got to be able to experience things.
—Linda Feldman, SITP Lead Teacher

It is exciting to be able to use art as a vehicle to teach all subjects. Art is not a separate planet. We can use it to explore so many aspects of the curriculum.
—Karin Baker, Lead Teacher—San Diego Museum of Art

During my 6 weeks of observation at SITP, I observed many lessons in which the arts (visual art, music, dance, and theatre) were actively infused or integrated into the learning at hand. As you read the following scenario, the story of the arts' role as a centerpiece for learning in SITP begins to unfold.

Scenario #1: San Diego Museum of Art Educational Classroom

(Museum Educators—Karin Baker, MOA Lead Teacher, and Dahlia D'Rosario)

Thirty enthusiastic third-grade students enter with backpacks and immediately go to small tables each labeled with five cities along the historical "Silk Road" (Chang'an, Kashgar, Baghdad, Tyre, Byzantium). The Museum of Art Education Classroom is richly decorated with three-dimensional bulletin board displays of the people, clothing, architecture, art, musical instruments, artifacts, and other cultural components of each of the five regions.

Museum Educator (ME): Where are we on our journey now?

Students: (enthusiastically) Kashgar!

ME: We left Chang'an China yesterday. How many miles did we travel by camel from China?

Students: (after some time and careful pencil to paper calculations) 2,200 miles!

ME: What kind of a math problem did we use to figure that out?

Student: We multiplied and then we added.

ME: Right! Keep in mind that it would take us 5 months by camel, so when would we actually arrive?

Students: (after even more figuring) In the summer!

ME: In Chang'an we saw architecture, clothing, and culture. What else is part of culture?

Student: Art.

Another student: Music.

ME: What about music?

Student: In cultures they have instruments. In Mexico they use guitars.

ME: Right! Today we are going to be learning about how we will see a change in culture on our Silk Road travels west. Let's review what we will see (vocabulary cards).

Students: *Symmetry* is about two sides being the same and balanced, *architecture* is about buildings, *agriculture* is the business of growing crops and raising animals for food.

ME: Let's go next door and see some photographs of Kashgar, our new destination along our Silk Road travels.

The students go to an open space in the next room to view a narrated PowerPoint slide program of a photographic journey to Kashgar. The slide show was organized to help the students imagine the experience of what a real Silk Road trip by camel might include—scenes of camel footprints in the sand, camel caravans, Kashgar regional landforms, desert and mountain passes, river valleys, horses and farms, agriculture, modern day people of Kashgar, marketplace, transportation, dances and festivals, costumes, arts, and architecture.

ME: (using a pointer with Freddy the Camel on the tip to guide the students' viewing) What kind of roofs do you see on these mosques? What are these towers called?

Student: There are domes on the roofs and (pointing) those are minarets. We have them here in the Park too. I've seen them!

ME: Yes, we do. Look for them as we walk to the Museum of Art to see the real art of China and view a large ceramic camel made in the eighth century.

As we made our way to the Museum of Art, the students were encouraged to find domed rooftops, minarets, and Islamic/Moorish ceramic tile designs. The third graders quickly identified that the skyline of Balboa Park was full of many examples tied to their study of the Islamic architecture of Kashgar.

Student: (When asked what we were going to see in the museum . . .) I don't know, but it's always a surprise and it's always cool! We find out a lot by reading the little cards near the exhibits.

I anticipated that the students might be noisy and a bit off-task during our visit to the Museum. Instead, the SITP student "artist/observers" were completely focused and quiet. Another museum educator commented first on "Guanyin," two statues from the 12th and 13th centuries.

ME: (inviting the students to gather near the statues with the information card labels) These are two life-sized statues from a country or area of the world. How do we know where they are from?

Student: You just read the label. Hey, they are from China!

ME: Yes, good. How old are the statues?

Student: 12th century. That means they are very old.

ME: What do you think they are made of?

Student: Wood, but they look like stone. How come?

ME: Because wood ages and takes the appearance of stone. These are Buddha-type statues. We might have seen them in caves during our travels from China. They are supposed to look friendly and wise and their long ears are a sign of wisdom. If you draw an imaginary line down the middle of the statues, are they symmetrical?

Students: (all move their hands down their middle vision field of the statues) No!

ME: So they are . . .

Students: Asymmetrical!

The students then travel to other pieces within the San Diego Museum of Art's permanent Asian Collection. Eventually, they arrive at a featured piece, eighth-century Chinese, a three-color glazed pottery statue from the Tang Dynasty. The students gather in a circle around this exhibit. Again, the class was completely focused on the exhibit. These young student artists knew a thing or two about camels—their mode of transportation during their Silk Road travels.

ME: Be a researcher. Where is this piece from?

Students: Eighth-century China.

ME: What kind of a camel is this? Do you remember? It has two humps.
Student: It's a bactrian camel.
ME: Yes, good. Is this a sculpture?
Student: Yes, because it has three dimensions.
ME: That's right. This camel was buried in a tomb in China and is over 1,200 years old. It is hollow. What colors do you see?
Students: Green, brown, yellow, and some drips down the sides.
ME: Yes, the dripped color was a technique used then. Take a really good look because we are going to make our own ceramic camels that we found during our travels on the Silk Road. Remember the colors you see and the way the camel is painted.

Back in the MOA classroom, the students were shown many pictures of camels in different poses. Then the museum educator guided them through an easy-to-follow, step-by-step hands-on process of making small clay statues of kneeling camels. (The next day the student art works were painted in the style of the museum piece.) The day's lesson concluded with math calculations of the distances traveled to Kashgar, work on an illustrated map of landforms and trading goods along the Silk Road, and journal writing about what happened during this imaginary journey.

The foregoing scenario vividly illustrates how art activities are integrated into SITP curriculum to enrich and augment student learning. The integrated activities used in this example served to make the study of the Silk Road immediate and real for the students. The Museum of Art offered direct experiences for students to view and discuss real art objects. Young learners were able to investigate, read, discover, and ask questions. Arts activities (in this case, visual art) were not isolated from the larger curriculum, but rather were used in active connection with learning through history, science, geography, culture, math, oral language, reading and vocabulary development, and writing extensions.

When asked about the integration of arts within SITP curriculum, Director Susan Wachowiak adds,

> School in the Park provides a unique point of view. Too often in education today, academic disciplines are taught in isolation from other subjects. So we teach math, social studies, science, reading, et cetera, without showing the interconnectedness of these subjects. At School in the Park, instruction is offered to help children make connections from one subject to another. The arts are a perfect example of this. Through art students can learn history, mathematics, science, narrative story telling, mood, setting, characterization. And this recognition allows students to integrate their academic knowledge with experience. Students gain a whole new way of looking at the world and realize that learning doesn't just happen at school. Because of this, I believe we are nurturing lifelong learning habits that will be with them the rest of their lives.

Through this immediate and experiential way of learning, students gained considerable insights into what may have been seen and experienced during Silk Road travels. In doing so, students were connected to the history of art pieces as well as their purpose and connection to culture. Because of their learning during the viewing of slides, discussion, question/answer, and visit to the museum, students were able to make powerful connections between past and present. Tangible evidence of learning could be heard during discussions, read in their journals, and seen in the delightful designs of the students' own ceramic camel figures, map illustrations, and journal entries.

The remainder of this chapter explores how the visual and performing arts (music, dance, theatre, and visual art) are imbedded and infused within several examples of SITP curriculum and instruction. Unfortunately, I found it impossible to mention every instance of arts within this unique curriculum. Instead, I have selected scenarios like the one cited to illustrate ways in which SITP students learn with and through the arts on a daily basis. As we read these we may come to understand what students, educators, and others involved in SITP already know—*that the arts can and do make all kinds of learning exciting and memorable.*

Setting: Background of Integrated Arts in Education

Children respond actively and joyfully to nonverbal communications and creative avenues of expression the arts provide. In order to nurture this natural excitement about an important way of learning, SITP students receive regular instruction involving activity in the arts. Furthermore, SITP arts activities are standards based and comprehensive in their educational design and exist within integrated instructional contexts across multiple content areas.

A comprehensive arts education includes doing and making art(s) as well as learning about the arts. According to the California Visual and Performing Arts Framework and Standards in the Visual and Performing Arts, children should have frequent and regular opportunities to produce their own works of art; observe artists and performances; examine, discuss, analyze, critique, and compare qualities of art; and by doing so, continue to explore their own and others' cultural heritage and connections to other learning (California Department of Education, 1996). Within the example given, we saw that Museum of Art educators purposely addressed each of these Visual and Performing Arts components in an integrated format within several content areas (history and social studies, geography, math, and literacy). As we see in the examples that follow, general education in the arts is a vital component, or core curriculum, imbedded within the larger SITP curriculum.

In SITP, curriculum activities in the visual and performing arts are linked to national state standards that include the following learning opportunities for all students:

- Increasing artistic perception including the processing of information about elements found within the arts;
- Creating and performing art;
- Analyzing and valuing through learning to make informed judgments about the arts;
- Learning about and making connections between the arts within their historical and cultural contexts;
- Comparing and connecting learning within the arts with other subject areas. (California Department of Education, 1996; MENC, 1994a)

Solid rationale for the value of infusing the arts within general education can be found within Eric Jensen's definitive compilation of research about the arts and their effect on brain development, *Arts with the Brain in Mind* (2001). Here, Jensen summarized research findings linking arts activity to other learning by concluding, "The arts enhance the process of learning. The systems they nourish, which include our integrated sensory, attentional, cognitive, emotional, and motor capacities, are, in fact, the driving forces behind all other learning" (p. 2). In SITP, education with and through the arts occurs actively and consistently within a variety of teaching and learning contexts. *Simply put, the arts are purposefully woven into the holistic design of SITP curriculum.* What is important here is that in SITP curriculum, education in the arts establishes its importance as a valuable way of thinking, learning, doing, and knowing in connection to many content areas and curriculum themes.

Another important factor woven throughout the SITP curriculum is its intentional focus on creative and alternative ways for all English language learners to participate and learn. When students are asked to imagine, observe, draw, act, sing, create, move, and listen and respond nonverbally, they have a variety of ways to actively express themselves with and without language. Students feel and are successful because they enjoy the opportunities to express themselves in new and creative ways. Not surprisingly, the results of infusing a variety of total physical involvement in creative responses to the learning at hand insures heightened student focus and participation as well as more meaningful and memorable learning experiences for all students (Hancock, 2000; Jacobs, 1989, 1997; Lapp & Flood, 1992; McDonald & Fisher, 2002; Rosenblatt, 1978, 1995; Vygotsky, 1962, 1978). Or, as simply expressed in the words of one enthusiastic SITP student, "This is fun. I hope we can learn like this ALL the time!"

Assessments of VAPA standards are purposefully imbedded in experiential arts activities and are largely authentic and active in nature (Burz & Marshall, 1999). In other words, when SITP students are invited to actively participate in the making of art, music, dance, or theatre, they can then be assessed in terms of what they create, perform, or do. Most arts experiences include a product. A work of art is created by individual students or groups of students and can be viewed and critiqued by teachers and other students through rubrics, out-loud discussion, and student reflections written in individual journals. There are multiple examples of forms of authentic assessment, discussion, and written assessments woven into the following scenarios of Arts in SITP curriculum.

PERSPECTIVES: EXAMPLES OF LEARNING WITH AND THROUGH THE ARTS

(Note to readers: The complete curriculum for all the museum arts activities mentioned in this chapter and photos of selected student artworks are available on the SITP Web site—schoolinthepark.net. Refer to the "Kids Corner" section of the Web site to view artworks.)

I would like to offer the following selected classroom observations and conversations to explore SITP contexts in which the arts are a centerpiece for learning:

Scenario #2: San Diego Historical Society Education Classroom

(SD Historical Society Director of Education—Sherrin Landis, and Museum Educator—Kim Vukasovich)

The following observation was of a lesson during a unit of study about the indigenous people, the Kumeyaay, and the natural resources of the San Diego County area. During this unit, the students study the history, culture, traditions, customs, language and communication, and arts and values of that culture. The students examine and discuss artifacts and historical photos and develop vocabulary about the Kumayaay to use in writing to be placed in their own "culture boxes." They observe and sketch the native landscape in the Park and also collect natural materials to make their own "useful objects" based on what they had learned about the Kumayaay. This day's lesson was about "How People Live and Believe" and was about culture and traditions.

ME: (playing a Kumayaay rattle) What do you hear? What do you think this is and what was it used for?
Student: A rattle... for dances....
Another student: To make music and dancing.
ME: Right. Remember that we talked about how rattles were made. (Plays an authentic recording of Kumayaay rattles and singing.) What do you hear now? What sounds do you hear? Who is singing? (Students identify a woman's voice.) Is she singing alone or with others? Are there times when we use music in our culture? (The students offer many examples from several cultural traditions most familiar to them—Mexican, Vietnamese, Laotian, African-American, Somali—as the Museum Educator lists all their ideas about holidays and celebrations.)
ME: Here is a photo of Eagle Dancers who may have used these rattles in music as they danced. (As the students look at the historical photo, one child becomes very excited and raises her hand....)
Student: Once, in class, we read a story about when the elders were dancing and wearing feathers too! (Their classroom teachers smile and nod in approval of the connection made to their reading in social studies.)

The arts of any culture provide a wealth of material for study. Within this short vignette, we again see how content-area study in SITP comes alive through direct sensory experiences provided by museum educators. The social studies/literacy unit about the Kumeyaay becomes real to students. In it they pay attention to and are focused on what they can see, hear, touch, and smell and construct. The students' hands-on exploration and guided investigation of artifacts and historical photographs, listening to instruments, singing and story-telling, viewing and collecting of natural materials found within the immediate environment, and hands-on construction of "useful objects" all serve to powerfully connect students to the history and culture of the Kumeyaay.

As we read in the example, these kinds of direct, meaningful interactions with the learning at hand can result in connections to what students are learning in their regular classroom. During the latter part of this SITP lesson, one classroom teacher read part of a story to a small group of students about how food was gathered and prepared by the Kumeyaay. As she read, the students were invited to pick up a variety of baskets, cooking tools, acorns, pine nuts, and grinding stones placed on the table in front of her. At appropriate parts of the story, the teacher allowed time for the students to touch the objects and answer questions about each. In this way, the museum educators' teaching techniques and styles actively influenced the classroom teacher's interaction with her students. When asked about this unit, this classroom teacher commented, "All the hands-on study is really wonderful. Our kids really need that. This is how they learn."

Scenario #3: San Diego Zoo Educational Classroom

(Zoo Educator—Judi Bowes)

The educational room of the San Diego Zoo is a charming and colorful setting for a variety of integrated arts activities connected to the active study of animal life. The classroom has a huge paper tree trunk and branches in the center of the room that become convenient places to hang a variety of student artwork. Within the zoo curriculum, the students learn about animal adaptations tied to survival (physical and behavioral), animal habitats, ways animals communicate, and simple classification through specific observational skills and data collection.

The students are actively engaged in constant observation of animals both in the classroom and in the world-famous San Diego Zoo. Judi Bowes, Zoo Educator, teaches observation through visual art. "I combine art and science through observation. I ask the students to slow down and really notice things. 'Notice' is my favorite word. If you draw it, you remember it and learn it. You don't have to know English well to show what you have observed and learned." Judi's goal is to have a visual perception element for everything she teaches. She ascribes to the educational philosophy that learners should be engaged in total physical response and thereby active in their scientific observation.

In describing her classroom unit about salamanders, Judi talked about how the students learn to observe salamanders, view photos of the animals, read books and stories about salamanders, then create beautiful drawings. Judi described how she brings a salamander to the classroom to use during directed drawing activities. In this guided art lesson she encourages the students by asking them to first "Draw a large S." The students are encouraged to carefully view the salamander from above in a "bird's eye" perspective. She prompts the young artists by saying "Did you notice the skin on the legs? Take a closer look. What do you see?" The students take a long look at an actual salamander and sketch what they have learned to carefully observe—size, shape, proportions, skin, legs, tail, head, eyes, feet, and so on. In these superb drawings, the students' incredibly detailed interpretations of salamanders are then placed within their sketched habitat, again reflecting the learners' understanding of where and how salamanders live.

During their animal life study, SITP students use movement and role playing to learn about animal behavior. Storytelling is frequently used during classes to share fables and folk legends about animals in various cultures. On the way to the zoo observations, students sing delightful call and response songs and chants about animals. All these activities serve to enhance students' understanding and enjoyment of learning about animals.

As I accompanied one class to the Reptile House of the San Diego Zoo, I was amazed at how on-task they were as they completed their hefty, clipboard data collection assignment. The SITP students were to find and classify all the reptiles (which I learned included lizards, snakes, turtles, and crocodilians) in each exhibit—a tall order indeed. I was a bit uncomfortable during this adventure because I have always intensely disliked snakes. However, I became more and more comfortable and relaxed as I delighted in the students' innate curiosity and excitement in finding each of the animals. They then helped me (not as astute in finding well-hidden animals) to find and actually enjoy viewing each reptile. I helped the students try to read each description displayed. For example, we were all soon aware that a "red dot" meant the reptile in that exhibit was poisonous.

At one exhibit, a student tugged at my arm and said, "Wait a minute. I'm going to stay here a while. I want to study this longer. Look at the cool eyebrows on this lizard." I thought he was kidding, of course. Then, when I slowed down and really looked, there was a small desert lizard with many rows of fascinating horned "eyebrows." The young scientist saw what I could not see. He had learned to see animals through the eyes of an artist.

Scenario #4: San Diego Junior Theater

(San Diego Junior Theater Education Program Manager—Bryn Fillers, Jr.; Theater Educator—Billy Ratz, Jr.)

The imaginative Junior Theater curriculum focuses on developing basic skills and vocabulary in drama through a themed unit tied to the California gold rush. Creative movement and active learning are at the heart of student discovery in these classes. The students have many opportunities to learn from the theatrical skills of teaching artists who model movement, characterization, and other skills with mesmerizing expertise. Literacy skills are highly stressed throughout the unit through many activities using oral language development (discussions/acting/improvising), reading, and writing.

SITP students participate in warm-ups and games to learn the tools of acting using body, face, voice, imagination, and teamwork. They experiment with ways to make sound and to move and how to attach emotion to each. They learn to project their voices and use expression and inflection. Pantomime is explored through games (Imaginary Ball, Emotional Musical Chairs, etc.) and improvisations. Character action and storyline (plot) are explored through connection to the study of historical gold rush characters and stories. Through this study, SITP students learn to develop a story or journey of a character they create (through action and writing), thereby developing a sense of empathy and timelessness with their characters and the life struggles they endured. Music, choral reading, geography and map skills, and math are also imaginatively incorporated throughout the unit. The students have opportunities to visualize, imagine, speak, move, write, and act as characters within the gold rush period.

At the end of their unit on the gold rush, the students create a performance piece about life in 1848 based on their writing and class activities (pantomime, choral poem, improvisations). They are encouraged to become "believable characters." Costumes and music are added. The production is videotaped and includes each student expressing how his or her gold rush character's journey ended. The students then view the videotaped performance and tell the person seated to their left that they did a good job. Then they turn to the person seated to their right and do the same. Then they say it for themselves!

For many of the SITP students, the Junior Theatre's California gold rush unit may be the first time they have explored learning through movement and character development. It may be the first time they used their imagination to create dialogue and action based on an historical period. They become delighted to express themselves in new ways and to imagine what life was like in another time. Even if their students have not as yet actually studied the gold rush period in their regular classroom social studies curriculum, many classroom teachers find that when they get to their own classroom units about this period of California History, students remember *everything* they learned in the Junior Theatre curriculum. Students remember dates, facts, geography, mining techniques, the woes of travelers, characters, places, and stories.

One classroom teacher said that in social studies her students now "continually want to act things out like they did at Junior Theatre. They are forever suggesting that whatever we are studying could become a play! They say, 'Let's just act it out!' " In summary, whereas we all know the saying, "All the world's a stage," it may be appropriate to add . . . "and we never forget what we do and learn while on that stage." Theatre educates.

Scenario #5: San Diego Museum of Photographic Arts

(Museum Educators—Vivian Kung Haga, Director of Education; Nora Shields, Chantal Legro, and Jennifer Fuller)

The design of this highly creative curriculum focuses on visual arts through the medium of photography and its history. Entitled "Light Writer Expedition," the first week of rotation develops student vocabulary and perception of the elements of visual art found in the art of photography. During this first week, the students create various works of art, look at the history of photography, and learn to analyze and critique their own work. According to the MOPA curriculum guide, "The first week will be a solid foundation of photography." As always in SITP curriculum, other subjects are infused into arts activities and vice versa. In the "Light Writer Expedition" students are engaged in reflective writing and the science of photography. They visit current exhibits housed in the Museum of Photographic Arts. Visual literacy is woven into the curriculum activities of this first week.

The goals of the week are charmingly presented to the students via a creative DVD filmed and acted in by MOPA educators. Students are instructed that they will face a number of challenges as Cadets in the Light Writer Academy. Challenges include proving they are responsible so that they can use a digital camera to produce an image. The students are also challenged to create and write. Their images and writing will be placed in a book for the class to keep. The book will be presented to their classroom teacher at a Light Writer Graduation Ceremony and they will, if they meet the challenges, receive a Light Writer Diploma!

At first, students learn to use Polaroid cameras and experiment with how to "frame" photographic images by taking pictures inside. The students then get to look at and discuss different types of cameras and learn about positive and negative space and contrast. They experiment with the effects of light on photosensitive paper and create Sun Prints. Students then learn about photographers and their craft, explore concepts of vantage points, use viewfinders, write about the kind of "Light Writer" they would like to be, and visit Museum galleries to view, discuss, and learn (visual literacy). Later, they learn about subjects for photographs, the concepts of close-up, long shot, worm's eye view, and bird's eye view, and create a collage that uses background and subject. Then the students break into groups and go to the park with a teacher to take one photo. Test shots are then projected for the entire class to view and critique.

The learning in this first week then proceeds to the study of photographic illusion and creative activities in which students are shown photographs and then asked to come up with a name for the photo. They are also given scenarios and must then come up with an explanation of how a certain picture was taken. After all this, they then go to the park and shoot their final digital image, which is included in a book and presented at the Graduation Ceremony for Light Writer Training by the director of MOPA, Arthur Ollman.

In the second rotation of MOPA, students focus on moving pictures. They also incorporate elements of theatre, dance, music, literacy, and visual art. Their main goal is to create and document their own DVD of a traditional Bantu tale, "The Name of the Tree." The MOPA educators first present the folk tale through puppetry (with the music of this culture) and students discuss how they might re-create their own scenes of this story. They plan how to direct and act and actually film their project. SITP students make masks, poster advertisements about their DVD, and costumes. They are the actors and directors and camera crew for the end product. The large puppets first introduced by the MOPA educators are again used in this final project that is filmed in the park. The whole process culminates with a gala premiere in the MOPA theatre complete with statuettes, sparkling cider, and awards. The MOPA staff lines the hallway as the students make their way to the theatre to applaud each and every one of the young filmmakers!

In viewing a beautiful DVD of one class' production, I was struck by the creative abilities of the students to readily incorporate all elements of their photographic study. Each scene reflected knowledge of these elements gained through hands-on experimentation. SITP students gained visual literacy through museum visits, learned how to critique their own and others' work, and increased their perception, understanding, and vocabulary about photographic arts. The direct application of learning about photography and moving pictures was realized in this DVD. Simply put, they learned by doing. They learned to be artists by being artists and creating art. More importantly, they learned they could do it by actually completing their own project with organization, group effort, and discipline.

Student memories of this exciting project are vivid, even after several years. When asked about their memories of SITP arts, a group of middle school students responded in the following ways:

"I remember learning about all the arts because we made our own DVD at MOPA. We got to act and film and everything. It was way cool."

"We got to design and make a publicity poster about our DVD."

"Once I learned how to do it, I've made my own movies at home. That's what Steven Spielberg did when he was a kid! I want to be a director when I grow up."

Ways to Get Started

Readers may read this book and throw their hands in the air and say "That's fine for SITP with all their Balboa Park resources and Price Charities financial support, but this would never work in my community!" There may be a temptation to conclude that arts in the SITP curriculum only work because of their unique support base and museum settings. We might look at these fabulous programs, museum educators, and SITP leadership as a special situation unique to this particular program. We might see the impossibility of duplicating these special circumstances in our own communities. However, as with any visionary approach to experiential education, arts in SITP had to have had a starting point.

SITP Director Susan Wachowiak, Lead Teacher Susan Feldman, and several museum educators offered the following starting points for others who seek outside expertise and resources to create or enhance the integration of the arts within schoolwide curriculum:

- *Background:* Review the ways in which SITP integrates the arts into their curriculum across several content areas. Visit the SITP Web site (schoolinthepark.net).
- *Join others:* Create a small team of teachers, parents, administrators, and others who are interested in working together to create meaningful, standards-based collaboration using community resources in your area.
- *Brainstorm:* Make a list and investigate places (historical buildings and sites, libraries, museums, exhibits, theatres, music venues, art galleries, dance studios, community colleges and local universities, etc.) that might serve as resources for experiential learning for students. Remember the goal is to expand outside the school walls to bring the real world into your curriculum. This requires some thought.
- *Know what you are looking for:* Before investigating outside sites and resources, carefully think about existing curriculum. Consult content standards in math, science, social studies, language arts, and visual and performing arts (VAPA), and determine what parts of existing curriculum you would like to enhance with and through the arts. Start simply with two or three *standards-based* curriculum themes (e.g., unit on indigenous people of your area that could be enhanced with local historical society photographs and artifacts, unit on an artist or photographer linked to permanent exhibits in your local art museums, math unit about shapes and geometry linked to local architecture or quilt displays, etc.). Think of ways this learning can be assessed and evaluated. You will want to know how to clearly articulate the learning outcomes of your program.
- *Visit local museums and other sites:* Once you have a solid plan, visit several possible resource locations in your area. Bring your list of standards-based curriculum themes with you. Ask to speak to the site's education director or individual in charge of the collection and have them take you through the exhibit and resources. Share your curriculum ideas with them. Let community resource individuals know that you are interested in "more than a one-time field trip for students," rather, a short *series* of visits (two or three) where students can learn through the resources and people there in collaboration with classroom teachers. If they are interested, meet again to create possible experiential curriculum as partners in this process.
- *Plan experiential curriculum to include an end product for the students:* Seek input from others to include a structured student project, production, or other end product during their educational experiences at a community resource site. Allow for community resource educators to also

visit classes and teachers at school sites. An end product will assure that the activities learned will have a goal and will allow you to bring the end product of that learning experience to your school site for others to see. The excitement generated by creative student projects will be considerable.

• *Spread the word:* Let parents, district administrators, content area coordinators, and school board members know about what you are doing. Include information in school newsletters and communications with parents. Ask the museum or community resource partners to do the same and publicize in their communication with patrons and members of their organization. Display student projects and photographs of the learning experiences within your program at school-site open houses. Ask your local paper and television station to do a featured story on your program. Invite parents and others to visit your community experiential learning sites when the students are there.

• *Evaluate:* Don't be afraid to evaluate and change your original ideas. Experiment with several curriculum ideas and outside resources. Ask for input from students, parents, classroom teachers, museum educators, school administrators, content area district coordinators, and others. Your program will evolve as the years go by. Try new ideas and constantly reassess.

• *Funding: Grants, private donors, philanthropic organizations:* Once you have clearly established goals, examples of student projects, and learning outcomes, find out where to apply for grants. Ask your school site principal and district curriculum coordinators for information about funding sources. Visit local philanthropic organizations in your area and ask to present your program to members there. Explore local fundraising options with your school-site Parent–Teacher organization.

POSTLUDE

This chapter has explored ways in which the arts are effectively and beautifully integrated within SITP curriculum. It is my hope that you will consider the value of augmenting existing arts education programs in your school or district with similar kinds of integrated, experiential learning in your own community. *All* children deserve regular instruction in the arts. Many school sites have a music teacher; some are also fortunate enough to have a teacher of visual art. Most school sites do not have theatre or dance teachers. Some school sites may actually have no arts programs at all. Why should we accept this situation?

Although we know our children need and deserve specialized instruction in all four arts, funding is often not allotted for this to take place. The classroom teacher then becomes the teacher of the arts for many children, particularly in underserved inner city schools. It is this group of devoted teachers who need the support, collaboration, and expertise of community arts educators to augment the delivery of quality integrated arts curriculum and learning activities for every child.

The SITP curriculum has served as a powerful catalyst for the delivery of more arts education at Rosa Parks Elementary. Based on their SITP experiences, the classroom teachers at Rosa Parks have sought ways to actively infuse more arts within their own schoolwide curriculum. Eleven classroom teachers voluntarily serve (with seven other middle school and high school classroom teachers) on a K to 12 Integrated Arts Curriculum Team. Since 2001, this team of educators has created and taught original integrated arts curriculum, collected resources for teaching, and presented lessons and units to teaching peers at all three Collaborative Schools (Rosa Parks Elementary, Monroe-Clark Middle School, and Hoover High School). The team has also exhibited student work from these original integrated arts units at the San Diego State University Love Library. These curriculum exhibits can be viewed at the following SDSU Web site: www.infodome.sdsu.edu/about/depts/spcollections/exhibits.shtml

Finally, arts education within SITP curriculum is an ever-evolving educational process. We anticipate this marvelous program will continue to develop. The beauty of the collaborations between Balboa Park museum educators, SITP leadership, San Diego Unified School District administration, SDSU/City Heights Educational Collaborative, Rosa Parks Elementary administrators, and teachers, parents, and others serves as lasting and powerful testimony of what can be done to insure every child participates and learns with and through the arts. Through the effort of many, the arts are indeed a "centerpiece" of learning in SITP. No pun intended, picture that!

REFERENCES

Burz, H. L., & Marshall, K. (1999). *Performance-based curriculum for music and the visual arts: From knowing to showing*. Thousand Oaks, CA: Corwin Press.

California Department of Education. (1996). *Visual and performing arts framework for California public schools: Kindergarten through grade twelve*. Sacramento, CA: Department of Education.

Hancock, M. (2000). *A celebration of literature and response: Children, books, and teachers in K–8 classrooms*. Upper Saddle River, NJ: Prentice-Hall.

Jensen, E. (2001). *Arts with the brain in mind*. Alexandria, VA: Association for Supervision and Curriculum Development.

Jacobs, H. H. (1989). *Interdisciplinary curriculum: Design and implementation*. Alexandria, VA: Association for Supervision and Curriculum Development.

Jacobs, H. H. (1997). *Mapping the big picture: Integrating curriculum and assessment K–12*. Alexandria, VA: Association for Supervision and Curriculum Development.

Lapp, D., & Flood, J. (1992). *Teaching reading to every child* (3rd ed.). New York: Macmillan/McGraw-Hill.

McDonald, N., & Fisher, D. (2002). *Developing arts-loving readers: Top 10 questions teachers are asking about integrated arts education*. Lanham, MD: Scarecrow Press.

Music Educators National Conference. (1994). *Dance, music, theatre, visual arts: What every young American should know and be able to do in the arts: National standards for arts education*. Reston, VA: Music Educators National Conference.

Rosenblatt, L. (1978). *The reader, the text, the poem: The transactional theory of the literary work*. Carbondale, IL: Southern Illinois University Press.

Rosenblatt, L. (1995). *Literature as exploration* (5th ed.). New York: Modern Language Association.

Vygotsky, L. S. (1962). *Thought and language* (E. Hanfmann & G. Vakar, Eds. and Trans.). Cambridge, MA: MIT Press.

Vygotsky, L. S. (1978). *Mind in society: The development of higher mental psychological processes*. Cambridge, MA: Harvard University Press.

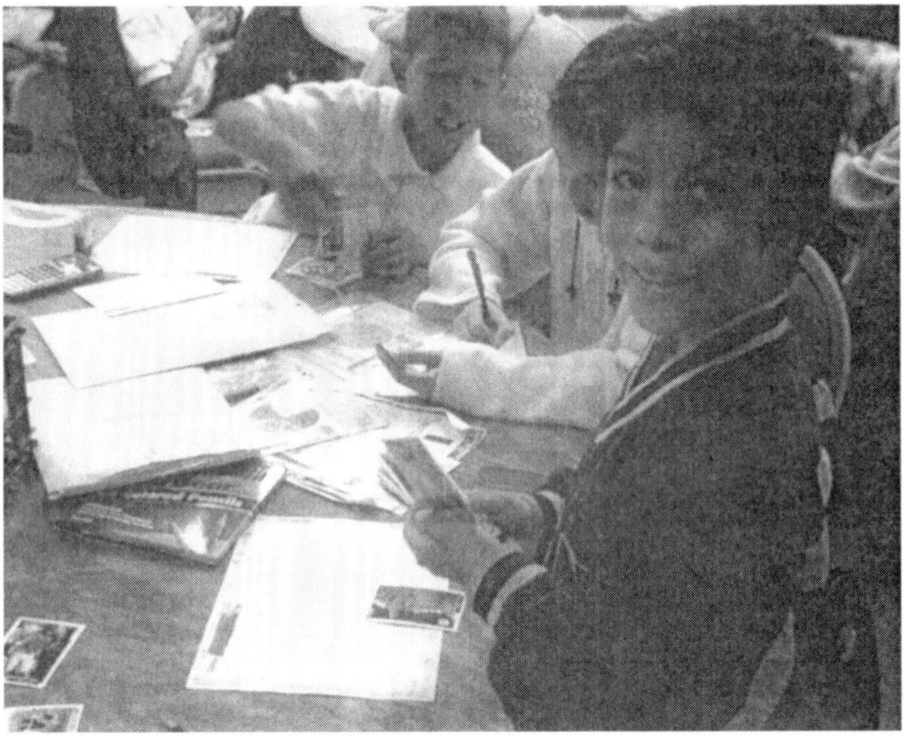

CHAPTER SEVEN

Where Is the Mathematics? Everywhere!

Kate Masarik

When asked, "What is mathematics?" most people answer with terms such as numbers, rules, fractions, decimals, area and volume, measuring objects, or difficult, or "I don't like math." There is, however, more to mathematics than just rules and operations; it provides the necessary tool to model and understand our world.

What do you think about or notice when you see this leaf? Do you think, "It is the color of fall, the seasons are changing," or "Oh-oh, I need to rake the lawn!" Or do you see the symmetry of the leaf; how the left side of the leaf matches the right side of the leaf; how the veins of the leaf form angles (the veins form linear pairs (adjacent angles whose sum is 180 degrees); where it appears as if one of the angles is twice the size of the other; and if you look carefully the same angle pattern appears to be repeated as the veins get smaller at each level. Do you notice how some of the veins appear to be parallel?

Mathematics is also about how we build roads, houses, and everything we make; why some objects are more pleasing to the eye than others; or how we can make predictions as to what may happen in either business or nature. "Mathematics affects everything from the food we eat, to the investments we make, to the size and shape of the cities we build. It provides the tools for coping with the technology that increasingly penetrates our lives" (Steen, 1990, front flap).

We live in a technological world where anything seems possible. Consider the movie, *The Matrix* in which the world the people interact with is formed by a computer program that translates 0's and 1's into objects and movement, a "virtual" reality. If 0's and 1's can become a world in which we can interact, how can we help students see the mathematics in the real world in which they live. If students are to realize the impact and importance mathematics has in their world, teachers must make evident to the students that mathematics is more than counting and number facts, or recognition of geometric shapes, and the application of mathematical principles in the classroom. Students also need to see the mathematics that makes up the world they live in, such as the growth patterns in nature, the steepness of a slide, why something is pleasing to the eye (symmetry, proportion), how board games are designed to be fair, and the list can go on.

A part of mathematics is learning how to work with numbers, but mathematical knowledge also includes knowing what the numbers represent; for example, understanding the amount off a price (discount); using patterns to explain natural phenomenon and business trends; analyzing and interpreting the data from a survey to uncover the likes and dislikes of a particular product or in determining the location of a new school; predicting patterns of growth of a city, and understanding the influence technology plays in our lives both at home and in the workplace. Understanding and being able to participate in this mathematics requires the participants to have problem-solving skills, different strategies to approach problems, ability to support conclusions, and being able to communicate their ideas to others. To develop problem-solving skills, students need to "be able to communicate and justify their solutions, starting with informal mathematical reasoning . . ." (Curriculum Development and Supplemental Materials Commission [CDSMC], 2000, p. 11). "Mathematical reasoning cuts across all strands" of mathematics, and mathematics is part of all that we do (CDSMC, 2000, p. 4).

Mathematics reform stresses the contextualization of the mathematics. As teachers, we can bring "real mathematics" into the classroom; however, we cannot forget to include the mathematics outside of the classroom, such as a geometry nature hike to look at the patterns of the veins in leaves and a similar pattern in the branching out of tree limbs; being able to determine the area and perimeter of the layout of safety mats under the playground equipment; or comparing the angles of slides for different age groups. The School in the Park (SITP) program, developed by the combined efforts of the staff at Balboa Park and Rosa Parks Elementary (under the direction of the City Heights Educational Pilot), provides the students multiple opportunities to study mathematics in the world outside the classroom. Using the students' experiences in the SITP, I want to point out not only the obvious mathematics being used, but also the not-so-obvious mathematical experiences that teachers can tap into as they continue working with the students in the classroom across grade levels.

During a typical week at SITP approximately 200 students from multiple grade levels (3rd–5th) use the San Diego Zoo and the museums in Balboa Park to explore, art in the Museum of Art, man in the history of Man, visual arts in the Museum of Photographic Arts, and/or sports in the Hall of Champions. In whatever situation the students find themselves, mathematics is present—some students are analyzing the statistics of baseball players as they put together their fantasy baseball team as baseball managers; other students are studying the size, shape, and attributes of bones and artifacts to tell the story of past cultures as archeologists do; others are explaining the attributes and adaptations that animals made with respect to their environments as zoologists do.

Let's take a stroll around Balboa Park to observe some of the students' experiences and the not-so-obvious mathematics that exists in these experiences. Our first stop is the Museum of Man, where for the past week fourth-grade students have been learning and practicing some of the techniques used by archeologists to interpret their findings. We drop in on the last day of a weeklong program to observe what is happening and to speak to one of the participants. The following is a snapshot of the day.

Look What We Found!

It's Friday! All week long my fourth-grade classmates and I have been getting ready for this day. We are going on an archeological dig!

We watch as the young girl and her teammates eagerly wait to be assigned a dig site. Finally, the group is called and taken to their site.

I wonder what we will find? We have studied bones to determine age, health, and the gender of the person; looked at the characteristics of artifacts to determine the creativity of the people; checked fingerprints. Now we are ready to put what we have learned to tell the story of ancient cultures! We will approach the site carefully so we do not disturb or destroy any of the objects that are there. There may be bones, talismans, and other treasures that we have to uncover. It is exciting to be able to put our mathematical and reasoning skills to work.

The team listens carefully as the head archeologist outlines the many duties that need to be accomplished at the dig. After the directions are given, each team decides on a team leader.

My young friend tells me, *"I am the team leader!"*

The work at the gravesite begins in earnest. Each team member is assigned a duty. One of the team members makes a list of the artifacts and bones so the team does not lose anything; another measures and examines the bones to determine the age and health of the people. A third team member measures the artifacts and studies the quality and patterning in the work to determine the level of intelligence and creativity of the people. Another worker creates a permanent record of the dig site by sketching where the grave is in relation to the others. The worker checks the layout direction and the size and content of each gravesite. The team leader approaches me.

I see that you are observing us today, are you a reporter? Let me know if there is any information that you need. My team works well together, helping each other out if one has a question. But they will explain how they use the characteristics of the bones to determine the sex, age, and health of the person. We know we have two people at the gravesite; one must be a very young child because the skull shows evidence of soft tissue.

After an hour, with most of the data collected, the team begins to compare the bones from their gravesite with those that they had studied earlier in the week. The team double checks the data with each other using the various references handouts and charts that are displayed around the "graveyard." The students make tentative conclusions while still collecting more data. When all the data has been collected, the team writes their report. The report includes a description of the occupants of the grave and their culture using evidence from the gravesite to support their conjectures.

Where is the mathematics? The "obvious" mathematics is the use of various and appropriate measuring devices that the students use to examine and analyze shin bones, collar bones, phalanges, and skulls to make conclusions about the age and health of the occupants. By measuring the dimensions of the various artifacts and analyzing the complexity of the patterns, the students are able to determine if the artifact was a useful object or a decoration, which in turn aids in determining the creativity and development of the culture of the people. The students support their conclusions by citing evidence from the data that they have collected.

As the students take on the responsibilities of being an archeologist, they experience mathematical reasoning, forming and supporting conclusions based on evidence (a preview of the two-column proof in geometry), and threading together the many pieces to produce a whole picture of the situation. Looking at characteristics and citing evidence for conclusions in any subject area can be connected to the studying of the characteristics and properties of number, functions, and geometry shapes.

While working as a team, the students also decides how to approach the many duties they have, identify relationships and distinguish relevant and irrelevant information, help one another with the tasks, and discuss their ideas and reasons for their conclusions. Having the opportunity to develop and practice discourse for a specific area of study can be a model that is used as an example for students as they develop and expand their mathematical vocabulary and understanding of mathematical concepts.

But the young archeologists are not the only students who are using mathematics! Let's go to the zoo.

Camels, Elephants, and Bears!

Students begin their experiences at the School in the Park during the third grade. One of the first venues they visit is the zoo. We all enjoy looking at the animals, birds, and reptiles, but the students' experiences at the zoo are more than sightseeing. Depending on the day of the week, we may find a group of third graders examining various animals and how they adapted to their environments. For example, camels have large feet that spread out over the sand so they will not sink; the antelope have small hard hoofs that can handle the rocky places they must maneuver; and the polar bear's coat turns as white as its surroundings so it can camouflage itself. The students also consider the purpose of various characteristics found on different animals. The okapi, a relative of the giraffe, has a solid color on its torso for camouflage, but zebra-looking stripes on its legs so that the young can identify and follow its mother through the bush.

On yet another adventure in the zoo, the students identify the distinguishing characteristics of birds. Using the reference pictures atthe sites, the students compare what they see in the pictures to the birds in the exhibit. The students are developing their ability to notice the defining characteristics of a group of similar animals—coloring, markings, beak shape, and size of bird.

On another day we find the students involved in a detailed study of the similarities and differences between two mammals—the elephant and the camel. After visiting each animal and asking questions of the respective trainers, students go back to the classroom to identify similarities and differences between the two mammals using a Venn diagram to organize their ideas. When the class has finished the large group discussion, each student then writes in his or her journal their conclusions using evidence that supports his or her ideas.

Where is the mathematics? Although no numbers are involved, students are looking at a common element—feet—while determining why each animal's foot has unique characteristics to the animal. This can be likened to students studying numbers—different ways to represent a number, such as equivalent fractions. Or students can use the same idea when studying linear graphs, straight-line graphs. All straight-line graphs can be written in the form of $y = mx + b$, however, each line can have a different value for the slope, m, and the y-intercept, b. Although the graphs will be straight, the degree of the slope and where the graph crosses the y-axis will be unique to each set of values for m and b.

Looking at similarities and differences in mathematics helps students to understand the mathematical structure of different functions—linear, quadratic, and so forth. What characteristics do the different functions have in common? What are the characteristics that differ from one to the other? How do these characteristics show up when the data is represented as a graph, set of values, or symbolic representation?

One important overarching mathematical concept is to be able to analyze problems by identifying relationships, distinguish relevant from irrelevant information, and observing patterns. Providing the students the opportunity to look for the similarities and differences between animals in terms of adaptation to their environment, observing and recognizing distinguishing characteristics in animals or birds is grounding for looking at the defining characteristics of different sets of numbers (fractions, decimals, percents, and their relationship to each other) or the different types of functions that the students will study later on—linear, quadratic, exponential. The experiences of one situation can be used as a foundation and reference for the students as they make comparisons between sets of objects and mathematical ideas.

Just as we want students to make connections within the different concepts of mathematics, the students make connections among their experiences at SITP. While studying camels, some of the third graders identified the type of camel and then related information about the camels and its role from their studies about the "The Silk Road." "The Silk Road" will be our next stop in the park.

The Silk Road

In the Museum of Art, third-grade students embark on an adventure that includes the discovery of silk and a trade journey through eastern Asia known as "The Silk Road." The students experience the yearlong journey during their week at the museum. Using photographs and drawings of the

7. WHERE IS THE MATHEMATICS?

cities and areas along the Silk Road, the students study the style of buildings, the crops that are grown, and the culture of the people. The students are participants in their learning, offering their ideas and explaining their way of thinking about what they see. While considering the architecture, the students recognize the concept of symmetry, which they had explored and discussed at an earlier rotation in the park.

Now that the students have previewed the cities, they prepare for their journey. The students discuss what they need to bring along, and they chart their journey across the desert, mountains, and fertile valleys by making a map. The map includes a type of scale converting actual miles to number of squares to show the distance between towns, and thus the entire trip. The students use a square to represent 100 miles. The maps also include information about the landscape, crop-growing areas, forests, and desert, as well as many other characteristics. The students make picture representations for each characteristic, placing a copy of the representation at its correct location on the map.

Where is the mathematics? As the students look at the pictures of the art and buildings they discuss what it means to have symmetry. A student offers the idea of "balance"; the student goes on to say that, "If I draw a line the shape is the same on both sides of the line." Later when looking at a picture of Chang'an, a young man balancing on the top of a 6-inch pole, the students point out that the man is balanced but the picture does not appear to be symmetrical. The museum teacher points out the difference between asymmetry and symmetry and the students discuss how symmetry is more than just balance. The word balance in everyday language, although a way to describe symmetry, is really describing an action, whereas symmetry describes the state of the appearance of an object; it duplicates itself in some manner (reflection, rotation, or translation). Students experience a situation that aids in their understanding of the preciseness of mathematical vocabulary generated by the conversation in class. At the end of the week, the students design and make a tile with a symmetrical design, providing another opportunity to look at symmetry more closely.

When the students make their maps, not only do they experience scaling real life into a representation that is converting large numbers to a smaller representation, which is a foundation for the idea of proportion, but the students are also beginning to use representations for concrete ideas, which is grounding work for abstract representations of concrete situations (variables) in algebra.

As we leave the silk merchants traveling through East Asia we find another group of students very much in the present, exploring another method of travel.

Flying High

A short walk to the area behind the Aerospace Museum reveals a group of fifth-grade students testing their rockets. The class is divided into groups that rotate through various duties: One group readies their rockets for testing, another group uses stopwatches to calculate the length of time the rocket is in the air, a third group uses an angle finder to determine the highest point of the rocket's flight. One person from each group reports the data to the main recorder. When the students are back in the classroom in the museum, they analyze the data to determine the "best" rocket.

Another activity that the students pursue during the week is the construction and alterations of "safety cartons" to be used when dropping a breakable object. After the initial testing of the carton on Wednesday, the students use the results to refine their structures. After constructing the new cartons they are again dropped from various heights until the object breaks. Students keep track of the original carton and revisions that are made, including the reasons for the changes.

Where is the mathematics? Building rockets, determining the size and shape of its fins, and the rocket's fuel capacity along collecting the flight data of time in the air and height of the flight are examples of the obvious mathematics. The mathematics continues when the students return to the classroom. Using the angle found at the top of the flight along with right triangle geometry, the students determine the height of the rocket's flight. Students also study the relationship between the time of the flight and the height of the rocket to determine an approximation of the speed of the rocket. Then, looking at the structure of the rockets that the best flights the students can determine the characteristics of a successful rocket.

The students also design and build the three-dimensional shapes to determine the best shape that will protect a fragile object when it is dropped. The experiments that that the students conduct during the week are filled with mathematics: the use of measuring devices, the building of the cartons, the collection and analysis of the numerical data when the cartons are tested in the "drop," and the resulting changes in the structure of the cartons. The students support their changes in the structure of the cartons and can then retest their carton to determine if the changes did in fact what they were supposed to do, protect its fragile contents. Too often in the classroom students do not have the opportunity to experiment and make adjustments on their "solution," in this case the safety carton, to see if their alternations can produce a better product.

As we travel to our next stop, the Hall of Champions, I hear what sounds like "Batter up!"

Getting the Team Together

In yet another part of the park, fifth-grade students are becoming baseball "managers" putting together their "dream teams." Working in the Hall of Champions the managers determine the lineup of their respective teams for the big games on Friday. Using the raw data of professional baseball players (e.g., number of hits, number of at bats, number of singles, doubles, triples, home runs, and strikeouts) the students determine their team lineup. The raw data, however, makes it difficult to compare players, so the students turn the raw data into numerical forms that "even" out the data and allow them to make comparisons between players in the various categories. The students set up the necessary ratios; for example, number of hits compared to number of times at bat or number of outs compared to number of times at bat. After setting up the ratios the students determine their decimal equivalent and percents.

The students then construct the spinner that they will use on Friday for the fantasy baseball games. The museum teacher models the steps as the students follow along. The students convert the first statistic to a percent, then determine the size of the angle (percent of 360 degree circle) and finally construct the correct angle to represent a sector of the circle spinners. As the students finish the first sector one hears the "ohs." The student sitting next to me remarks, "cool." Then, with their partners, the students finish constructing the circle graphs that become the spinners for the game.

Where is the mathematics? Putting together the fantasy baseball team gives the students practice working with ratios, decimals, percents, and multiple representations of the same value. By using a common representation of the data the students can make direct comparison as to the talent or ability of the baseball players. In the process of converting the raw data to a common representation, the students discuss the meaning of each representation. For example, the students use ratios to describe the number of home runs to the number of at bats, 1:20, and the number of outs to the number of at bats, 1:8. The ratio 1:8 sounds favorable; it suggests that something happens more often. Since that particular ratio, however, describes the number of outs to the number of times at bats, a manager may prefer the 1:20 ratio instead. Such discussions acknowledge the importance of knowing what each term in the ratio represents and not just looking at the numbers.

In order to play fantasy baseball the students construct a spinner that reflects the probability of getting a hit, an out, etc. The students change the decimal notation into percents and then find how each piece of data can be represented as a sector of a circle (percent of the area of a circle in terms of degrees of an angle). Making the spinner by converting the decimal to a percent to a portion of the circle provides the students opportunity to explore probability through the discussion of what do you think could have happened.

Ms. Y, the teacher, remarked that the students had worked with decimals, fractions, and percents in the classroom; however, their role as baseball managers provided another opportunity to help solidify their expertise with these representations.

These are but a few of the experiences that the students have during their 3 years of rotations through the museums and zoo in Balboa Park. The students become archeologists, zoologists, scientists, silk merchants, rocketeers, and baseball managers. Each of the experiences is set up to engage the students in mathematics and its role in the different venues.

Behind the Scenes

The success of School in the Park is due not only to the enthusiasm of the teachers, museum personnel, and especially the students but also to the preparation work that is done. The lessons are carefully planned, based on sound pedagogy, and both the national (NCTM, 2000) and state (CDSMC, 2000) mathematics standards. The lessons are purposely designed so the students can interact with real-world experiences and that connections are made to the mathematics the students experience in their classroom. The teachers and museum personnel have an ongoing conversation concerning the mathematics being taught so connections can be made between the two sites. Both the teachers and the museum staff use the mathematics standards to develop and continually refine the mathematical activities that will help the students understand mathematical concepts.

The day's lesson begins during the 20-minute bus ride from Rosa Parks Elementary to Balboa Park. The teachers prep their students for the day's activities, reviewing the previous day's work, working on vocabulary, or having the students partake in an activity that relates to the work ahead.

At the park, as the students, teacher, museum teacher, and support staff travel to their respective museums, the students may be asked to point out symmetry in the architecture, distinguish between vertical and horizontal elements, or sing a song especially written to help them remember some of the ideas that they have learned. When the students arrive at the museums, the student and teacher discuss what will be happening and their role in the day's work. For example, preparation could include discussing what the students should be looking for, what the activity entails, reviewing both mathematical and nonmathematical vocabulary, and making connections with previous visits to the particular museum or related museums. The students then embark upon their work.

Within an atmosphere of adventure and learning students have the opportunity to work with "school" mathematics in the "real" world. For example, the third-grade students do not take notebooks along with them as they tour the zoo; however, there is a discussion beforehand and the students are given a number of things to look for and do, which they need to be ready to report on when they get back to the museum classroom. As the students look for similarities and differences between animals, they can later use those same skillswhen looking at the similarities and differences of two-dimensional shapes. The students come back to the museum classroom, discuss what they have seen and learned, and then write in their journals about their experiences. This writing helps in language development, making conjectures, and supporting ideas—a foundation for writing about mathematics and how they solve problems.

The teachers, students, and museum personnel are proud of their program and the work that is accomplished. A common comment made by all is the quality of the students' questioning skills, the development of their writing skills, their ability to observe and make connections between museum experiences, and between museum experiences and classroom work, and the application of the concepts in different situations. The teachers whom I talked with not only comment that the SITP relates the work to what is happening in school, but that it also provides common experiences that the teachers can refer to back in the classroom as they extend the students' studies.

A fifth-grade teacher who works with the same group of students from third through fifth grade has experienced the entire gamut of the SITP program, having participated in each of the museums and zoo. She remarked on the continued development and revisions in the program, the attention to standards, what is happening in the classroom, and the development of lessons that is ongoing and enriches the students' experiences. She also remarked on the students' continued references to the museums from year to year, remembering the past experiences relating them to new experiences whether in the classroom or at another venue. The students are engaged, inquisitive, enthusiastic, and bring up connections between their experiences.

I have provided only a glimpse of the activities that the students engage in during their experiences in the park—the visible mathematics, measuring artifacts, figuring the cost of lunch at the zoo, converting raw data to multiple representations (ratios, decimals, percents), measuring the altitude of a rocket flight. There is also the "invisible" mathematics, such as the making sense of the data, justifying the hypotheses, identifying defining characteristics, and writing about the experiences. Each of these experiences with real-life situations provides a foundation that the students can use as they move from arithmetic to algebra, or from measurement to formulas for area and volume of objects, or from map reading to plotting points on different coordinate systems.

Not Just for Here

Although the museum personnel and teachers and staff at Rosa Parks realize the uniqueness of Balboa Park and The School in the Park program, the participants in SITP are eager to point out that the philosophy behind this endeavor can be implemented wherever there is an outside facility—a local art gallery, historical society, museum, farm, business—as long as there is communication between school and the source with planning of the learning experience, prepping students, having the students reflect on their work, and providing opportunities and means to make connections not only among mathematical concepts but also between different areas of study. The idea of using facilities beyond the walls can be done anywhere if teachers, schools, and museum personnel communicate.

REFERENCES

Curriculum Development and Supplemental Materials Commissions. (2000). *Mathematical framework for California public schools: Kindergarten through grade twelve* (Rev. ed.). Sacramento, CA: California Department of Education.

National Council of Teachers of Mathematics. (2000). *Principles and standards of school mathematics*. Reston, VA: Author.

Steen, L. A. (Ed.). (1990). *On the shoulders of giants: New approaches to numeracy*. Washington, DC: National Academy Press.

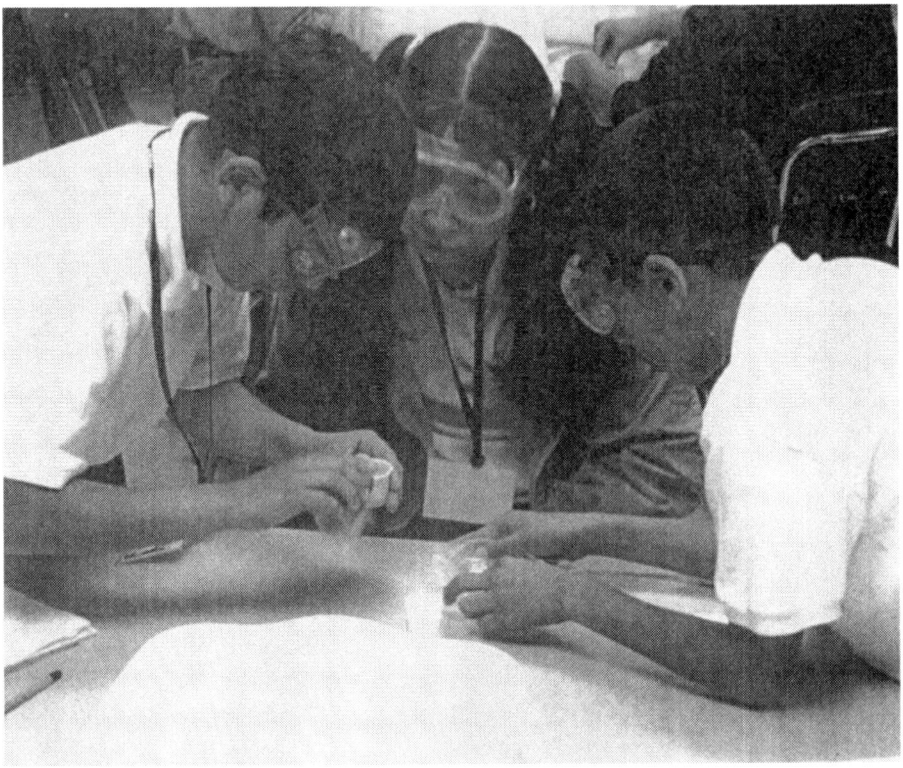

CHAPTER EIGHT

The Opportunity to Learn Science Like Scientists: Museums Are a Good Idea

Donna L. Ross

> *Humans are highly motivated to learn when they are in supporting environments, when they are engaged in meaningful activities; when they are freed from anxiety, fear, and other negative mental states; when they have choices and control over their learning; and when the challenges of the task meet their skills.*
> —Falk and Dierking (2000, p. 32)

Those of us who have taught for many years can recall instances when students become so engaged that they cannot *avoid* learning. At these times, students are so excited about asking questions, trying out new things, sharing their observations, and making sense of the world around them that it is nearly impossible to stop them, be it for recess, lunch, or to go home. These situations exemplify the motivation just described by Falk and Dierking (2000) and represent the pinnacle of good science education. Unfortunately, these occurrences of meaningful science learning are too infrequent in traditional school settings. The innovative School in the Park program, however, provides students with a large number of these science experiences. Teachers receive models of exemplary science education to use back at the school site and students gain far more than just an opportunity to be in a new environment. I was asked to visit School in the Park and think about the ways in which science standards were being met. In this chapter, I outline my thinking on this subject. I have invited Anson Lee from the Reuben H. Fleet Science Center to think about how School in the Park has impacted the museum and their educational curriculum. His response is included in Fig. 8.1.

The Reuben H. Fleet Science Center's curriculum prior to working with the School in the Park program was typically a series of demonstrative events that were intended to excite students about science and encourage investigation. This was reasonable in the beginning as the workshops only allowed 1½ hours per group of students. There was little time for students to construct meaning from activities and little or no assessment. Through our participation with SITP we have been able to facilitate more meaningful investigations where students can learn complex concepts through inquiry.

We strongly believed that if teachers were going to share 2 weeks of student time with us, we needed to make it as valuable as possible. We focused on the physical science standards for fifth grade. This was a natural choice being a physics-focused science center. The first week with Rosa Parks we investigate the physical properties of matter. The first investigation is very process focused to highlight skills that will be used throughout their experience at the Fleet. We then experiment with boiling and saturation points of various substances, combined and pure. Students are later given a box of objects in which they determine density, magnetism, electrical conductivity, volume, mass, color, and so on. Using their student notebooks from the investigation, students then organize the objects into a chart based upon their physical properties.

Chemical properties of matter are the concentration for the second week. Students investigate with calcium chloride, sodium bicarbonate, and phenol red to determine possible indicators of a chemical reaction. Students begin to identify physical from chemical changes. The culminating activity ties their experiences back to the periodic table where students identify physical and chemical properties of the elements and their organization.

We try to maximize all of the benefits from the collaboration. The shared staff allows experimentation with concepts such as boiling points. We try to push the envelope of a typical classroom considering the support and resources at our disposal. There are not too many fifth-grade teachers who can demonstrate the range of boiling points using liquid nitrogen. We utilize the floor exhibits whenever possible to help students hone observation and questioning techniques.

We also use the experience with School in the Park to demonstrate inquiry models in the classroom. Most of the investigations could be facilitated easily by one teacher. We have since modified the curriculum for teachers in the classroom.

School in the Park provides our staff with a working lab where we can continually expand our expectations for students and ourselves. It never looks the same from one class to the next, but we know it's always getting better. We only hope that we have had as much of an impact on the students at Rosa Parks as they have on us.

FIG. 8.1. Impact of School in the Park on Fleet curriculum. By Anson Lee, Community Teacher Developer, Reuben H. Fleet Science Center.

Student Engagement

Imagine a class of fifth-grade English learners immersed in science investigations at the Reuben H. Fleet Science Center. Their voices can be heard coming from a classroom in the back part of the museum. This is their third consecutive day here this week, but they were here for a week earlier in the year, and they have spent several weeks in two other museums this year. Each day they have some semistructured time to explore exhibits in the public part of the museum and some time to work in the classroom with a museum science educator. Today, the students are divided into groups and they have the overall task of examining different items to identify physical and chemical changes. The museum educator and the classroom teacher are in the room, but the student groups are working independently. The noise level is high, but it consists of productive, on-task talk. The voices are excited and everyone is eager to share. The students are huddled over various objects in the middle of the tables. One group drops an Alka-Seltzer™ tablet into a clear tub of water. The student discussions that follow were not prompted nor interrupted by adults.

"*Ahhhh . . . it is boiling!*"
"*It isn't hot. Does it have to be hot to be boiling?*"
"*Oh, it's going faster.*"
"*Look at all of the bubbles!*"
"*It looks like the bubbles are walking around on the bottom.*"
"*I think it is a physical change, because it is still water.*"
"*Maybe it isn't [just water]?*"
"*How can we tell?*"
"*We aren't supposed to taste it.*"
"*Well, I think it was physical when we broke it [the Alka-Seltzer] because it was still the same, just a different shape, but now, I don't know.*"
One student looks carefully at the water with a magnifying glass and says "*But the white is gone now. It isn't just a different shape.*"
"*I think it is chemical because the Alka-Seltzer goes into the bubbles.*"
"*Yeah, it isn't the same now.*"
"*Touch it. Is it hot yet?*"
"*No, it isn't boiling, just bubbling.*"
"*The bubbles are stopping, but the white stuff is still gone.*"
"*It's chemical.*"
"*Yeah, it's chemical.*"
The students turn to their science journals to sketch their investigation, record their observations, and state their conclusion. The student sitting nearest to me draws the tub with many bubbles, each of which has an arrow pointing up toward the top of the tub. He writes "It is chemical because it changes from the white to the bubbles and goes out into the air."

A girl on the other side of me writes "It is chemical because it changes and can't go back."

Another group is watching ice cubes melt. They discuss their observations of the ice as it melts.

"It is wavy."
"No, it is just melting."
"But that makes it wavy."
"It's like the edges go first."
"Yeah, it's softer."
"Smoother."
"It is a physical change because it is still water."
"Yeah."
"Yeah, because we could freeze it again."
"It's [the water] cold."
"It'll freeze your fingers."
"Just like the ice."
"It's [the water] almost out to the edge of the dish."
"I know it's physical. Let's do another one."

The group turns to their journals to draw the materials and write their conclusions. One student writes "I know this one is physical because all I need to do is put it in the freezer and it is the same." Another writes, "physical because ice and water are the same, they go back and forth."

Observation and Evidence

The National Science Education Standards (NRC, 1996) for K to 12 education in the United States identifies fundamental understandings that thread through all of the content standards. One of the foundational tenets is that "scientists develop explanations using observations (evidence) and what they already know about the world (scientific knowledge). Good explanations are based on evidence from investigations" (p. 123). In 1869, George Sand wrote, "The whole secret of the study of nature lies in learning how to use one's eyes." People, both children and adults, need practice making observations and then using that evidence to draw conclusions. Scientific observations involve patience and attention, and can include the use of all of the senses. They build on some of the same skills, such as comparing and contrasting, found in many language arts curricula. Drawing conclusions based on evidence requires logical thought and a willingness to explore alternative explanations. These high-level thinking skills support the students as they continue to study science, but they also cross disciplines to increase achievement in all subjects.

The national recommendations are directly aligned with the way the School in the Park students in the previous examples are learning science.

They are using their prior knowledge about chemical and physical changes, making observations, and developing explanations. The materials the students are using are not particularly unusual or innovative, but the approach is. The students are provided with enough time to really observe the materials, moving on to the next set of materials only when they are ready. Instead of glancing at the ice melting and moving past it because it is such a common sight, they consider how the ice and water are changing. They are encouraged to talk with each other and share their understanding of the investigation. The students know they are expected to provide evidence to support their conclusions regarding the type of changes they observe and they must ultimately be able to support their own conclusions. This approach to science learning much more closely resembles how scientists engage in science than most standard school science lessons. Can these labs be set up in the fifth-grade classroom back at Rosa Parks? Absolutely. Many of the labs can and should be set up in every classroom. Does the milieu of conducting these experiments in the museum labs with scientists add to the authenticity of the activities? Absolutely.

Authentic Experiences

The common approach to science lessons in schools is as follows: The teacher provides a scientific question, the materials, the steps to follow, the method to organize the data, and then expects the students to stay "on-task" and follow the steps. Often the teacher even provides the conclusions saying something like "Well, if you did everything correctly, you *should* have seen . . ." or "If we had time to finish, we *would* find that . . .". This approach decreases student motivation because the investigations are not authentic and evidence is not used to make sense of the phenomena. The students begin to view adults as the source of scientific knowledge and science as a series of facts to memorize instead of recognizing the wonder of developing an investigation, gathering data, and making sense of the new evidence in light of what is already known about the topic.

The explorations at the science museum focus on teaching science in a more authentic format. In general, the School in the Park lessons begin with prepared questions to spark the investigations, but as the students work, they can decide on the direction of the explorations. The students can develop new questions and, in some instances, design an experiment to answer their own scientific questions. As one of the School in the Park students said "I like science because it keeps you guessing. You don't know what to expect and there are always more questions to ask."

Connections to Prior Knowledge and Experiences

Over at the Museum of Man, fourth-grade English language learners are refining their observation skills as they learn about fingerprints. The museum educator asks them if they have ever watched any television shows in which detectives compare fingerprints to identify a criminal. This sparks a lively discussion about a television series centered on forensic science, *CSI*. The young female museum educator dramatizes an escape from a crime science and the students identify all of the places she touched. They excitedly call out, "the table," "the wall," "the projector." Then the science educator continues to explain that people leave behind a trail of fingerprints and DNA wherever they go. Before the students begin the fingerprint activity, they excitedly talk more about crimes, both real and on television, solved through forensic science.

One of the most effective ways to teach new information is to connect it with students' prior knowledge and to make real-world connections. Across the park, at the aerospace museum, an educator is making connections between the paper airplanes the students have created and the different historic planes the students were observing earlier in the museum. At the Fleet Science Center, the science educator is making science accessible by using concrete materials that are familiar to students, including ice and magnets, to introduce abstract chemistry concepts. These museum educators, with the help of the classroom teachers, have engaged the students in the content by making connections to shared knowledge from the media, the community, the museums, and personal experiences.

Breaking Stereotypes

Back at the Museum of Man, the museum educator continues by discussing how people obtain jobs in forensic science. She talks about college science courses and how fun college can be. She says, "College is great. You can choose your classes. If you really like science you can choose to take lots of science classes. You can choose the time, too. You can take classes at 8 in the morning or 2 in the afternoon. One semester, I didn't have any classes before noon. You can study with cute boys and girls and flirt with them between classes." Again, the buzz of excitement is palpable. I hear students saying "I wouldn't take any classes in the morning." "I'd take all science and P.E. classes." "I'm going to be a scientist like on *CSI*." "I'm going to San Diego State." "Me too and I'll study only with the hot girls!" College, careers, and science are topics of animated discussion. The federal government has launched a large effort to increase college-going rates in underrepresented populations (Gear Up) and NSF, among others, regularly supports research to increase girls' interest in science. At the School in the Park, mission accomplished! Classroom teachers can encourage future college attendance, but the younger museum educators and college work–study museum docents are more credible and can serve as role models in a way the teachers cannot duplicate.

One of the challenges that science educators face is confronting tightly held stereotypes about who can be a scientist. Many people carry a mental image of scientists as geeky White men or wild-haired mad scientists. The media tend to perpetuate these biases, even in otherwise educational programs. Most urban children of color do not know any scientists personally, and many people, adults and children alike, can only name White, male scientists. The School in the Park program introduces inner-city children to many different scientists and presents the biographies of diverse scientists. In addition, the museum educators tend to be young and personable, a far cry from the stereotypically boring nerd in a white lab coat. The possibility of studying science becomes cool or "tight." This is especially important for girls. Research has shown that girls' interest in science wanes around fourth grade. In middle and high school, girls are less likely to take science electives and tend to do less well compared with boys in required science classes. However, when science connects with girls on a personal level, when the curriculum relates to the girls' real-world experiences, and when role models are similar in age and ethnicity and have familiar backgrounds, girls are much more likely to report positive perceptions of science and the desire to continue their studies in science.

Vocabulary Development

Another recommendation for effective science instruction is to engage the students in concrete experiences prior to focusing on the subject matter vocabulary. Once they have the background concepts, the vocabulary becomes necessary and memorable. Over at the Aerospace Museum, small groups of fifth-grade students are launching rockets made from 2-liter bottles. They are studying aerodynamics, Bernoulli's principle, and the importance of controlling variables. However, the vocabulary they are using is informal. At this point in the investigation, the students are discussing the "cone" and the "back part of the rocket." The scientific language is provided to the students only as the context creates the need. In this way, the students have the schema to make sense of the new vocabulary and to increase retention.

Engaging the students with the concrete materials before introducing the scientific vocabulary is particularly appropriate for English learners. This format is less threatening and they can concentrate on learning the science before the language. Then, as the students encounter the need for new vocabulary, they have a context for the language and will be more likely to use the terms correctly in the future. The museums are rich in language. The vocabulary is present on posters and charts in the museum classrooms, and the exhibits in the public portion of the museum reinforce the learning.

Discipline Integration

At the San Diego Zoo, third-grade students are making a graph of animals that live in different biomes; at the Aerospace Museum, fifth-grade students chart their results for the rocket launches; at the Natural History Museum, fourth-grade students diagram the processes that create different types of rocks; and over at the Fleet Science Center fifth-grade students draw the apparatus as they make observations. Teaching science is really a multidiscipline event. Many of the skills and processes used in science are crucial to language arts and mathematics learning, as well. For example, graphing, categorizing, diagramming, labeling, comparing, summarizing, contrasting, and identifying patterns all cross subject boundaries.

One of the most effective ways to integrate language arts and science is through science journals. Students learn that scientists keep journals of all of their experiments, questions, and observations. As students begin to keep journals, it is useful to provide them with prompts. However, it is important to keep some of the prompts very open-ended. Science is all about developing questions and if the prompts are too guided, the students will not develop their own hypotheses or design their own experiments. Inquiry-based science is centered on the students' asking questions, designing experiments, choosing materials, and analyzing their own results, but it does require scaffolding the instruction to assist students in scientific thought.

For example, in an experiment with paper airplanes, fifth-grade students might be given a few of the following prompts:

My airplane flew _____ meters.
I was surprised when my airplane _____.
I wonder if my airplane would go farther if I _____.
The plane that went the farthest looked like this _____.
The one thing I changed on my plane for this try was _____

In the fourth graders' rock investigation at the Natural History Museum, prompts could include:

I think _____ are igneous because _____.

I wonder what causes the rocks to _____.
The two rocks _____ and _____ are similar because _____.
What would happen to the rocks if I _____.
The _____ rock reminds me of _____.

Lifelong Learning and Background Knowledge

In interviews with parents, several shared their beliefs that School in the Park was the best program for preparing students to continue learning, "perhaps even in college." They view School in the Park as a chance for their children to have the same opportunities and background experiences as more affluent families. It is an issue of equity, and the parents see this as one of the few times their children are on an equal footing. They told me the children come home talking about all kinds of things they, themselves, have never seen or experienced. The parents believe the program builds their children's English vocabulary and makes them understand how to continue to learn in all different settings.

Volunteers and employees of the museum voiced many of the same thoughts, as well as mentioning how seriously the students view the opportunities. One college work–study student commented that the School in the Park classes treat the docents with "respect and appreciation." She said, "Other students come in and run around and treat us like servants." The difference is "obvious as the School in the Park students read the exhibit information, walk, discuss the science, and ask me questions." The other classes come in and "run around pushing buttons without knowing why." The classroom teachers also reported how much more comfortable the students seem in unfamiliar settings after their first year of the School in the Park. "They just have more confidence and poise. They will be museum-goers for life. They see it as normal now."

Teacher Benefits

Interviews with the teachers who bring their classes to School in the Park indicate that they receive the most help with their teaching in the area of science. Several teachers told me "I would never have tried these units on my own." Others confessed, "I really don't teach much science except when we are going to be coming to the park." The assistance with curricular decisions is valued, but so are the materials. "The Natural History Museum is one where it would be really hard, impossible really, to do the same hands-on activities at school without the exhibits." Every teacher I interviewed mentioned some version of the following statement "There are just so many materials so easy to access here. I know I can do a lot of it at school, but the kids really need the experiences they get in the museums. They haven't ever seen these things before." One teacher commented, "They become so passionate about things I would never have thought about. We go back to school and research all kinds of things." Many teachers mentioned their pleasure at seeing the students reading about a science topic they had covered at the museums. One teacher described a student who would rarely sit still or focus on anything. "It is amazing, really. He becomes so engrossed in the experiments, I actually forget about him and that NEVER happens. He has started coming to me and telling me about books about airplanes he is reading . . . and he used to hate to read!"

Several of the classes spend the afternoons, after the museum visits, extending investigations and coming up with new questions for the museum educators. One teacher said, "I try to get them to think of all the questions they can while we have the advantage of an expert." Many said, "I've learned so much myself."

For many elementary teachers, science is not an area of strength. Most teachers feel that their own background is not strong enough to teach science well. Others cannot imagine how to incorporate science into their program. Overall, hands-on science is too often neglected in the elementary curriculum. The School in the Park program models science instruction, provides the teacher with content knowledge and resources, and provides compelling evidence that science can be a strong motivator for students to read and write.

Independent Thinking

Back at the physical and chemical changes investigations at the Fleet Science Center, one group of fifth-grade students looks at a shiny piece of steel wool and a rusty piece of steel wool to identify if a physical or chemical change was the cause of the difference in appearance. I overhear:
"What is this?"
"It smells."
"Ugh."
"Is it iron?"
"I don't know. Are they the same? Does this one smell, too?"
"No."
"Something changed."
"Duh. It looks different."
"Do you think it is iron?"
"This one sticks [to the magnet]."
"Does the other one?"

8. LEARN SCIENCE LIKE SCIENTISTS

"It sticks, but only a little bit."
"They aren't the same, this one is all fluffy."
"And this one is falling apart."
"But the shape is the same."
"No, it isn't."
"No. Look it's all broken apart."
"That's just because we ripped it apart. It's physical."
"Like the paper." (The students had been shown a piece of paper being ripped as an example of physical changes.)
"Maybe it is physical because it just changed color."
"But this one stuck to the thing [magnet] and this one didn't."
"Yeah it did."
"No, that was only because it was caught on the other one."
"Look, it sticks."
"Part of it, but not here."
"Try the magnet here."
"Let me see."
"Most of it doesn't stick."
"Is it chemical? Is it chemical? People, people, I said, <u>is it chemical?</u>"
"Yes."
"No."
"I'm writing yes."
"No, it isn't because it still sticks and it is just a different color."
"This one gets all icky all over your hands."
"Yuck."
"That's because it is chemical."
"No, it is just dirty."
"I'm writing chemical."
"We don't have to all write the same thing."
"Yeah, we just have to have a reason."

As a science educator, I find this exchange very exciting. These students may not know yet what caused the change in the steel wool, but they are having an authentic discussion of their observations. The students are listening to each other and responding to their peers, as opposed to waiting for an answer from the teacher. They are using their prior knowledge and their sense of smell, touch, and sight to synthesize evidence in order to form a conclusion. Ultimately, they recognize that they do not need to agree, but they need to be able to articulate a rationale for their answer. These inner-city, elementary school English learners have a better scientific approach to a question than many high school students. In fact, when these students reach high school and are studying oxidative reactions, they will have strong background experiences to draw on.

The Essence of a Scientist

I love fool's experiments. I am always making them.
—Charles Darwin, 1887

Curiosity is the trademark of a true scientist. We ask questions even when everyone else assumes they know the answer. This foundation of the scientific approach is evident at the Fleet Science Center as another group looks at a system consisting of two batteries in series, connected to two test tubes positioned upside down in rubber stoppers. There are small bubbles forming in one of the test tubes. I overhear:

"*This one [test tube] has a lot more bubbles.*"
"*It is going faster in that one.*"
"*The bubbles are going up and making a big bubble.*"
"*Why?*"
"*Maybe it is just smaller.*"
"*Can we take it off and see?*"
"*I'll do it.*" (*The student takes the tubes out and compares them.*)
"*No, they are the same.*"
"*Then why aren't the bubbles the same?*"
"*Maybe the red one [wire] has more energy.*"
"*How could it?*"
"*Maybe it is longer.*"
"*Take it off and we'll see.*"
"*Will it electrocute me?*"
"*No, try it.*"
"*It's just a battery.*"
"*Here, hold it next to the black one [wire].*"
"*Put this [the clip on the end] next to the same thing on the black one.*"
"*Hold it straight.*"
"*They are the same.*"
"*Put it back.*"
"*Are we making electricity?*"
"*Yes, I think it is electricity from the batteries.*"
"*Then it is boiling from the electricity?*"
"*No, it isn't hot.*"
"*But there are bubbles.*"
"*Did it stop when we took it [the wire] off?*"
"*Yes.*"
"*Would it go back so there isn't air in the top [of the inverted test tube]?*"
"*Try it.*"

"I think it was just air before, I think it is something different now."
(They disconnect the wires.)
"It's stopping."
"Look. It is stopping."
"But it isn't going back. It's staying."
"So if it doesn't go back does that mean it's chemical?"
"I think it is chemical because it is electricity."
"Switch the things [wires] and see if it makes a difference." *(The students switch the black and the red wires.)*
"There, it is the plus sign that makes the bubbles."
"Now more bubbles are going to the other one [test tube]."
"Is it the plus side or the red one [wire]?"
"We already looked at the red line, it must be the plus."
"But we know it doesn't go back. The air stays up there at the top."
"So it is chemical."
"Yeah."

As a science educator who frequently visits classrooms and works with science teachers, I often have seen similar activities to support students as they learn to identify chemical and physical changes as part of a chemistry unit. Typically, students look at the apparatus, declare it to be chemical and move on. This group of students, however, shows the curiosity that defines the essence of a scientific mind.

The discussion illustrates the level to which these students are lacking English vocabulary, as well as some fairly basic scientific concepts. This is common among underserved English learners who have had limited background experiences. Yet, despite the holes in their prior knowledge, these students have asked more questions and explored the material in more ways than groups from highly affluent schools. They still need practice in controlling variables and recording their data, but they have the willingness to experiment. They have learned that in science it is okay, even necessary, to try out their ideas. In the science education literature and among professional development circles, the phrase "inquiry-based science" is in vogue. These student-centered questions and investigations are vital to inquiry-based science.

A Good Idea

In 2000, Falk and Dierking, authors of *Learning from Museums*, described their prediction for schools of the future. They suggested that schools will recognize the value of informal science education and exploit the museum and aquarium resources. They wrote "If, and probably more accurately when, schools finally accept the inevitable and reform their practices, they will be a force to be reckoned with. They will greedily snap up any and every good idea they can find, including the museum concept. Don't be surprised to see future public schools built around museums" (p. 230). The City Heights Collaborative has done more than snap up this good idea, they have improved it. Better than simply exploiting the resources, they have formed a partnership in which the museum educators have been nudged to improve the semiformal educational programs and the teachers have been inspired to expand their vision of exemplary instruction. The three-pronged approach to science education, including museum exhibits, inquiry-based museum education programs, and follow-up science instruction at the school complement one another to create an environment in which students learn the scientific concepts, recognize the real-world applications of science, and begin to break down stereotypes about who can do science. A good idea, indeed. The evidence, including my observations, support the hypotheses with facts, reasonable assumptions, and more questions. This is good science!

REFERENCES

Falk, J. H., & Dierking, L. D. (2000). *Learning from museums: Visitor experiences and the making of meaning.* Walnut Creek, CA: AltaMira Press.

National Research Council. (1996). *National science education standards.* Washington, DC: National Academy Press.

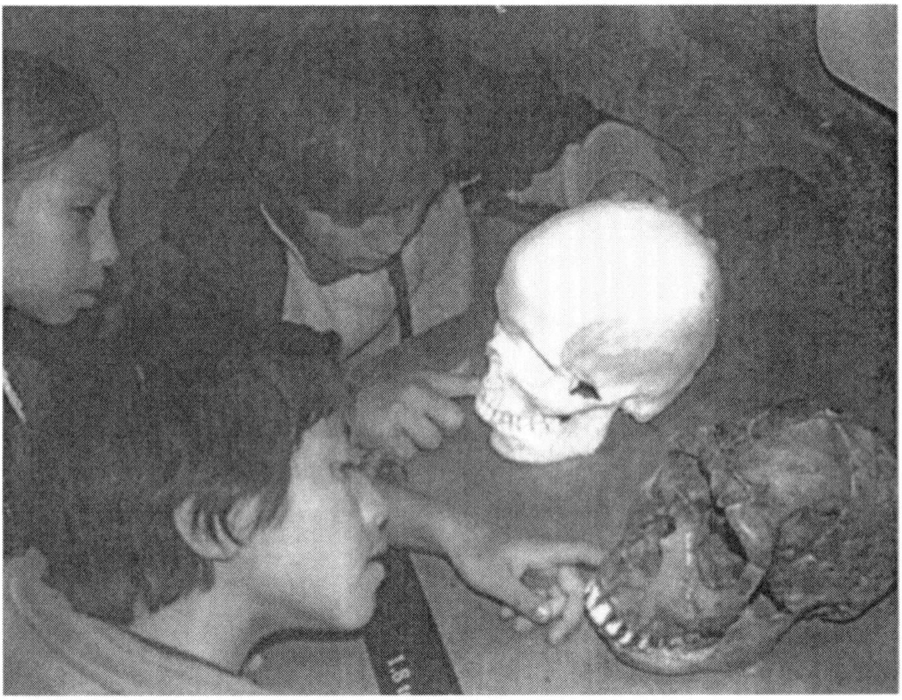

CHAPTER NINE

Engaging Students in Social Studies Through Exploration, Documentation, and Analysis: Museums and Field Studies Can Bring Social Studies to Life

Emily M. Schell

Through the Eyes of Students

Cindy: Social studies is my favorite! I like to learn about Native Americans, their tribes, where they lived, and how they had lots of things. Pretty soon, we get to make a village, but first we have to learn a little bit more. But this week, we have to travel to all those places [pointing to a wall-size map of the Silk Trade Route] in our imagination. When we use our imagination, we can see where we are going and what's all around.... I see robbers, markets, people who trade—merchants—trading tortillas, fish, and white silk. I see boats, camels, silk in purple, red, green, and blue. Did you know that only kings and queens in Byzantium could wear purple silk? I have to write that in my poetry journal.

Alexis: Merchants. That's a new word. Hey, look on the map. There's a shoe! Next to the Arabian Sea and the Red Sea. Arabia. It's a shoe! [giggles from several students]

Cindy: That's right. Now we have to write.

These third-grade students are engaged in focused, social studies–based conversations while mapmaking and adding to personal journals during a week of studies at the San Diego Museum of Art. This week's explorations transported them to a time long ago and to places far away. Using their fertile and vivid imaginations as vehicles, students traveled along the Silk

Trade Route between China's Changan and Greece's Byzantium to trade, learn, and then share their findings with others.

As a visitor, I listened to Cindy while she continued coloring and labeling her map and then turned to her poetry journal. While she spoke, my mind was full of questions. *Are these new terms for her? How much does she really know about merchants and silk? Did she just say Byzantine?* I thought of the many seventh-grade students who are struggling to learn about this period of history and don't even attempt to pronounce such names as Byzantium, much less learn about the city's importance to trade, growth, and expansion. I could tell that Cindy was proud of her perfect pronunciation as well as her grasp of this new knowledge. While writing in her journal about her final stop in Byzantium after her weeklong travels along the trade route, Cindy whispered to me, "In my poetry journal, I'm calling it Istanbul." Understanding that Istanbul is today's name for this important trade city, I realized that Cindy had transported herself back to the 21st century through her journal, exercising both wit and wisdom.

Cindy was not the only third-grade student immersed in her studies at the museum. Her classmates were eager to share their thoughts and experiences after an exciting week "traveling" along the Silk Trade Route. Fortunately, they had all documented their sights, thoughts, feelings, and new learning in their personal journals. At the week's end, their teacher Patty Osborne gathered the students together and invited each one to share his or her favorite entry. Some entries reflected the anxieties and dangers of those who traveled along the route, whereas others reflected the optimistic and adventurous spirit of seeing new sites, meeting different people, tasting strange foods, and acquiring new treasures. The entries shared held several elements of a great novel or motion picture. I felt myself transported back to a time and place that was foreign and exciting. All entries were well received by the class and the teacher because they were all rich with adventure, intrigue, new vocabulary, historic context, and individual personality. In all, these students shared an amazing adventure into the past where they grew in their understanding and appreciation of transportation, geography, economics, technology, animals, art, cultural exchange, and history.

Experienced teachers know that these kinds of in-depth, practical understandings of important history and social science strands call for coordinated lessons and meaningful experiential learning. In other words, similar outcomes would not be a common expectation after a typical field trip to a museum, even with some classroom support. These third-grade students gained a greater understanding of universal concepts, such as trade, transportation, and culture, as well as new knowledge about specific people, places, and events in history. This occurred as a result of their experiences during their second rotation to the San Diego Museum of Art.

These students had experienced the first rotation at this museum earlier in the school year when they studied color, line, shape, texture, and dimension as part of the School in the Park Program. The coordinated, experiential lessons for this week built on students' prior learning in the art museum and in the classroom, and invited students to learn through museum resources, literature, maps, PowerPoint slide lectures, guided visualization (or imaginary travel), and collaborative activities.

On Monday, students were introduced to the Asia Crossroads exhibit in the art museum and explored a central feature—a large map identifying the historic route. The students then moved through the exhibit with museum educators to view up close, analyze, and discuss the artifacts, including Tang ceramic camels, a silk dragon robe, bronze vessels, a jade comb, and carved red lacquer boxes. They were left with such questions as *Where did these things come from? Are these items valuable? Why? Who made them? For whom were these things made? What were they used for? How old are these items? Do we have things like these today? What makes these artifacts so special?* With curiosity piqued, these students were prepared for a week of exploration, documentation, and analysis—important ingredients for successful learning.

In their classroom across from the museum, students revisited a large wall-size map of the Silk Trade Route. Displaying similar information as the professional, detailed map in the museum exhibit, this handmade map provided a more colorful, interactive, and inviting approach for these young learners. It was the kind of map they might be used to seeing and using in a classroom on a bulletin board. A movable camel was fixed on the map to identify the various locations, or "stops" along the Silk Trade Route. Each day, as the students moved along the route, they moved the camel, too. Learning stations in the museum classroom reinforced and enhanced what students saw in the actual museum exhibit, and provided opportunities to correct misconceptions, ask questions, and gather more information. The classroom also provided a place for literature books, including a favorite titled *Stories from the Silk Road* (Gilchrist, 1999), and other hands-on tools for the teachers and students. While this classroom environment supported the exhibit, which was just a short walk away, the actual exhibit remained close and accessible during the week.

Students were placed in travel groups to work together cooperatively as they studied, participated in trading activities, completed sections of their travel maps, and wrote in their journals each day. At the beginning of the week, students were given a list of items that they should have at the end of their travels (at the end of the week). So, trading wisely each day throughout the week was encouraged. Considering the dilemma of many elementary teachers who struggle to teach basic economic concepts, I watched as students conducted cost-benefit analyses, made choices, and applied their understandings of supply and demand in the context of this historical period and setting.

Each day, as students "traveled"—from Changan to Kashgar to Baghdad to Tyre to Byzantium—they learned about the history, geography, art, and culture of this place through a series of activities. The structured activities took them from place to place, both physically and figuratively. There was productive movement of bodies, ideas, and focused conversation between the museum, their classroom, and other sites to see and use in the park. Again, considering the primary grade teachers who struggle to teach basic geography in their classrooms, I witnessed the themes of movement, location, region, place, and human–environmental interactions applied in what the students did and learned. Reinforced with meaningful maps and personalized activities for students to record their movements, observe landscapes, and discuss observations, geography was alive and well in this week's lessons.

Integrating some of the cultural elements of their travels, students enjoyed stories read or told by their teachers and they sampled treats, including dates and other sweets. Students participated in the arts as they stopped along their route and, for example, in the trading city of Kashgar, discussed the importance of their camels before making ceramic figurines of camels. Learning in the style of Tang artists, and replicating artifacts seen and discussed in the museum exhibit, students drizzled green and yellow glaze over their camel figurines. Stopping in Tyre, students learned about tile art that adorned public buildings. The students viewed examples found on buildings in the park before they returned to their art studio/classroom to replicate colorful symmetrical designs on tile squares of their own.

Reinforcing the importance of colorful dyes used on silks and tiles, and bringing poetry into the "mind's eye" of these imaginative students, Mrs. Osborne wrapped up their week at the art museum by reading poems of color from Mary O'Neill's (1990) book *Hailstones and Halibut Bones*. After reading, visualizing, and discussing these colorful poems, and after celebrating the trade route travel journal entries of the students, Mrs. Osborne invited students to write colorful poems of their own. This activity transported her travelers, her poets, back to their 21st-century classroom where they all met the following Monday to share their poems, their memories of their week on the Silk Trade Route, and their ongoing adventures in learning about life here and now, as well as far away and long ago.

Viewing this week in the park as an adventure of sorts, students were united in their experience, but "saw" and learned different things. Some, like Cindy, were anxious to get to the park for this week on the Silk Trade Route because she had heard so much about this exhibit and program from her older brother. I found this to be the case with several students whom I met throughout the School in the Park program. Because of what a sibling, a cousin, or a friend had told them about School in the Park, students were anxious to experience this for themselves. Imagine that—students talking about their social studies lessons outside of the classroom and in their homes/neighborhoods with such enthusiasm that other students are filled with anticipation for their turn to learn, too! That's the way we would like to see all of our lessons, isn't it?

Developing Content Knowledge Through Sound Practices in Teaching Social Studies

The Task Force of the National Commission on the Social Studies, funded by the Carnegie Foundation, the Rockefeller Foundation, the MacArthur Foundation, and the National Geographic Society, embarked on a joint project with the National Council for the Social Studies, the American Historical Society, and the Organization of American Historians to confront educational reform issues and provide practical suggestions to address the criticisms of social studies education in American. The task force produced a report, titled *Charting a Course: Social Studies for the 21st Century* (1989), which outlined 10 characteristics of a social studies curriculum for the 21st century. Following are five statements from the report, also viewed as goals for effective social studies programs, which describe ways that the School in the Park program promotes the development of social studies among students:

1. *Social studies provides the obvious connection between the humanities and the natural and physical sciences. To assist students to see the interrelationships among branches of knowledge, integration of other subject matter with social studies should be encouraged whenever possible.*

The elementary school curriculum, which is often seen as overcrowded and overwhelming, offers multiple opportunities for the integration of subject matter. The benefits of integrated instruction include relevant and purposeful learning of the "big picture" (Pigdon & Woolley, 1993) and social studies is often seen as the great connector among subjects for integrated instruction. With social studies topics or standards at the core of unit plans, the integration of literature, music, art, drama, science, and writing may be designed to enhance student learning and promote the application of knowledge and skills among the various disciplines.

The curriculum designed for School in the Park seeks to integrate standards and content for students at each grade level, while promoting the natural inclusion of social studies throughout the various museums. For example, fourth-grade students at the Natural History Museum, which can be seen as exclusively science driven, keep busy learning about the physical geography that has supported changing life forms over time. Students walk through the park and stop at vistas to discuss and sketch landforms. They bring geography to life as they experience movement over various terrains, learn and follow directions, and use such tools as a compass before relating these to maps. Science concepts of natural resources, plant and animal life, and geology are integrated into discussions, mapmaking exercises, and other activities in this museum.

Fourth graders also spend time in the Museum of Photographic Arts, where one might expect visual arts and technology to dominate the curriculum. Instead, while learning about and using digital cameras, students learn about the purpose and use of the camera as subjects, form, and perspectives are emphasized. Students study about character traits that can be captured through a photographer's lens and about the photograph as a method of documentation and communication. Students learn about the various roles and responsibilities of people, and about the multitude of choices that people have faced throughout time and place.

Through the programs in the park, students see social studies as multidimensional and all-inclusive. They are able to learn new information and skills while accessing and using prior interests, knowledge, and skills from mathematics, language arts, visual and performing arts, science, and social studies lessons. Complex as this seems in the planning of lessons, when students enter real-world environments through the park program, the complexity works for students who need to see the connections across the curriculum (Steffey & Hood, 1994).

> 2. *Content knowledge from the social studies should not be treated merely as received knowledge to be accepted and memorized, but as the means through which open and vital questions may be explored and confronted. Students must be aware that just as contemporary events have been shaped by actions taken by people in the past, they themselves have the capacity to shape the future.*

"We need different modalities to teach the content," explained fourth-grade teacher Shayne McCool, while her students wrapped up their week at the Museum of Man. "They learn a lot of things about landforms, Native Americans, archaeology, and evolution, but it's the little things that help them learn—the connections—that happen here in the park."

That word "connections" comes up a lot when talking to teachers about social studies. In this case, Mrs. McCool described a great deal of content that is "delivered" through this social studies program in the park, but honed in on the "hook" that helps students see the value in learning by connecting the information to their personal lives. "It's hard for students to make connections in class when they are reading the book and trying to remember facts," she explained. "But in the park, they have questions to take home and talk about at home. They have opportunities to explore things in the museum and with the museum educators . . . with each other."

One of Mrs. McCool's fourth-grade students, Roberto, helped to illustrate this as he reflected on his week of studies as an archaeologist:

> In the park, we always learn something new. And when you learn something new, you get a wrinkle in your brain. I got lots of wrinkles this week. I learned that when human bodies have diseases, it shows up on their bones. If you ever look at a skeleton, you can tell if the person was diseased when he died. . . .
>
> It's important to know about the past so people can know what happened back then and about the different cultures. Some information you won't find in books and written records, so you can find more information by looking at bodies. . . . I'm glad to have more information like this. Now I can teach this to my sisters and my friends. And to my mom and dad. They think the park is great because I get more knowledge, go home, tell them, and they learn something new, too. Today I will tell them that we did activities and learned how scientists handled artifacts and what we can learn from skeletons. I already told them some of this, but now I have more to tell them.

Many students stated that learning in the park was fun. Roberto was no different. He said that it was fun to study bones when you think you are an archaeologist and learn how to handle artifacts and tools properly. Roberto went on to explain that in the park, he gets to learn things that he was not going to learn at school. He knows that subjects, such as Egyptian mummies, are not normally part of the fourth-grade social studies curriculum in California. He said, "We get to learn things before the grade we're supposed to. When I get to sixth grade, I know I won't struggle as much when we learn about Egypt." I asked him how he knew that he would study more about Ancient Egyptians in the sixth grade and he replied, "My sister. She knew more in sixth grade because she went to the park in fourth grade, too." Roberto and his classmates feel better prepared for the lessons that await them in future grades, while enjoying current studies that simulate their experiences as historians, anthropologists, and archaeologists.

Furthermore, Roberto, like many other students learning in the park, has begun the process of shaping the future by reteaching what he has learned with others. Most immediately, students are taking home lessons to share with siblings and parents. The students have expanded their classrooms through assignments given by teachers (e.g., read your journal entry to someone at home; interview a parent to find out what brought him or her to San Diego; look for examples of artifacts at home), natural enthusiasm for their learning experiences in the program, and a desire to share knowledge that is new, interesting, and inviting.

>   3. *Reading, writing, observing, debating, role-play, or simulations, working with statistical data, and using appropriate critical thinking skills should be an integral part of social studies instruction. Teaching strategies should help students to become both independent and cooperative learners who develop skills of problem solving, decision making, negotiation, and conflict resolution.*

I met a fourth-grade student named Rosa at the Junior Theater in Balboa Park. She explained to me how much fun it was to learn about the gold rush during her week at the theater in the park:

> Social studies is really interesting. I learn cool stuff that my parents like to learn, too. I'm learning stuff that my mom and dad did not learn because, well, they did not go to school here [in the United States]. So I go home and tell them all about what I learn, like the gold rush. I show them my journal and they get to learn, too!

Rosa described, in great detail, the California gold rush. She used exact dates, names, and places to tell about the discovery of gold, the "big secret," the newspaper reports, and the people who came from around the world to claim their fortunes. Interspersed in her accounts were such questions as "Can you believe he started that rumor?" and "Do you know how much it cost to buy things back then?" Rosa was creating and exploring questions of her own after being presented with a variety of questions during her week of studies. She said that she has even more questions, such as "How did gold get here? Did it travel by space ship and land here?" Rosa's self-guided exploration has already begun: "The teachers told me gold is a mineral that is found in the Earth's crust, but I have to find out more about that."

While questioning, Rosa also made evaluative statements when describing what she had learned, including "The women's clothes did not match. That's because they did not have a lot of clothes to wear, and they saved the colors for festivals" and "I read a book last year in Spanish called *La Fevre de Oro* and I was confused thinking 'How could gold have a fever?' Now I understand about the gold fever and I think what I thought last year was funny." Rosa is self-monitoring her learning processes as she encounters new information and is challenged to reflect on what she already knows about subjects that are introduced through programs in the park.

Rosa's ability to do more than receive information about this historic period allowed her to access prior knowledge, connect new information to what she already knew, question what she was knew and was learning, and make evaluations about this information as well as her own learning. The structure of the program assisted Rosa and her classmates in doing these things as they learned. The fourth-grade students started their week listening to stories—based in primary sources of information—about the gold rush, then embarked on an imaginary journey to a place near Sacramento in the year 1849. After their guided visualization exercise, each student self-selected a role to play during the remainder of the week. "I chose to be a dancer. A lot of girls picked dancer. A lot of boys picked sheriff," explained Rosa. It was from these perspectives that students continued their studies of this period in history.

By the third day of the program, students learned about period clothing and dressed up in the kinds of clothes that someone in their role might have worn. Rosa shared, "I told my friends that I did not want to be living in that year. It was embarrassing—the clothes. But some of the boys looked good in a moustache." Rosa and her classmates were able to record some of these reflections in their daily journals. Additionally, students returned to their visualization journeys to imagine a loved one that was left back at home while these students, in their gold rush–era roles, went to California in search of gold. Rosa says she imagined having a husband and wrote to him in her letter "I missed him a lot. I told him all the things that I went through, like I went through a desert and swamps with alligators to get here. I had a lot of mosquito bites. I was very dizzy when we traveled by boat."

In her journal, Rosa was able to explore some of her questions that she held about the gold rush. For example, she told me that she wanted to know if there were any women who discovered gold. She said that there were mostly men searching for gold in her imaginary journeys, but she thought there had to be at least a few women in the mines or rivers. Rosa knew that she was in charge of her imaginary journey as it unfolded in her daily journal. So, by the end of the week, she wrote from the perspective of her gold rush–era character that she had found 60 big pieces of gold. She wrote a letter to her imaginary husband that she would return home in 1 month because she had found gold and that they were going to be rich! In sharing this story, Rosa couched, or justified, her unrealistic turn of events by revealing that one student in the class wrote on their first day that he had found 20 pounds of gold. "We all laughed," she recalled, realizing that her claim, as a woman, to 60 golden nuggets was improbable, but more realistic than her classmate's tale.

The imaginary journeys, journal and letter writing, and costuming culminated in the staging of a short play based in what students had learned about the gold rush. Lines were memorized, staging directions were learned, and acting techniques practiced. Rosa and her classmates enjoyed producing their play, then watching the videotaped production afterward. "We had lots of fun doing the play and we learned lots of stuff," said Rosa. "We did a play in third grade, so mostly we knew about acting. But we learned a lot more about the gold rush."

> 4. *Learning materials must incorporate a rich mixture of written matter, including original sources, literature, and expository writing; a variety of audiovisual materials including films, television, and interactive media; a collection of items of material culture including artifacts, photographs, census records, and historical maps; and computer programs for writing and analyzing social, economic, and geographic data. Social studies coursework should teach students to evaluate the reliability of all such sources of information and to be aware of the ways in which various media select, shape, and constrain information.*

Learning centers present opportunities for students to work and learn in small groups offering them more hands-on, one-on-one instruction with a focused topic. Third-grade students at the local historical society participated in learning centers throughout their week while studying about newcomers to San Diego. Working at different centers that changed with each day's era, students participated in a variety of activities to learn about newcomers to San Diego during subsequent chronological periods.

At the beginning of the week, students were given an overview of the week's activities that would take them into the historical society to learn from original documents, photographs, illustrations, news articles, posters, letters, and the like, and then into the museum classroom where they could use that information to learn more. The third graders were challenged to "be on the lookout" for particular people, places, and events that represented important periods in San Diego's history as well as the diversity of cultures that influenced the development of the local region. The class was divided into four learning groups and identified as either Architects, Horticulturists, Humanitarians, or Philanthropists.

On Monday, students rotated between learning centers that focused on:

a. Trade: Students were given various items from the different cultures and economic classes that coexisted locally in the 18th century. For example, students held either a piece of hide, a jar of salt, a piece of lace, a paper parasol, an iron, vanilla beans, spices, a willow basket, or a piece of fabric. After analyzing and discussing what some of these items were, how they were used, and who might want or need them, students began to work together to trade items. During the process, questions erupted and students wanted more information about the items, the people who lived here, what society valued, the accessibility of certain items and materials, how items were transported, and what contextual materials existed (e.g., Did they have sewing machines? What could be made from a hide? What can you do with vanilla?). Students learned that bartering is a skill in making deals, and that a great deal of knowledge was required to determine the values of items. When students ended up with items after trading, the teacher at the learning center explained more about each item and its relative value during this period in history.

b. Cooking: Realizing that food was important during this, and every, period in history, students spent time at this center measuring and mixing ingredients to make a food staple for many newcomers—biscuits. During the process, the teacher guided students in their thinking and discussions of food and nutrition, access to and accuracy in measuring ingredients, and the historical context of both. Skillfully, the teacher guided students in their thinking about food and nutrition between their present world and that of long ago when there were no refrigerators, supermarkets, microwave ovens, and food processors.

c. Chores: A natural connection to the cooking learning center was this center where students learned about the multitude of jobs that were necessary for children and parents to complete on a daily basis. Here, students made butter while singing period songs and brainstormed stories and games that could be used to pass the time. All the while, one student churned butter in the wooden replica of a butter churn and the others shook glass jars of butter watching the butter-making process in motion. Students alternated turns at the wooden churn, but otherwise never stopped working. Some said, "This is easy! I could do this all day!" while others shared, "Not me! This is boring!" All listened as their teacher told amusing stories about life on a farm, milking cows, and cats coming 'round to eye the butter.

d. Shopping: This learning center featured a variety of imported products from China that piqued students' curiosities and generated a number of questions about what items were used for, how much they cost, and who bought them. Students simulated a mini shopping spree as they realized there were a finite number of items to purchase that had varying costs and uses. This hands-on time allowed students to analyze some items that they had only seen in photographs or drawings, and to raise questions. Students became curious about what resources were used to make the items and noted the ingenuity of the people who made these items. Recognizing the endurance of some items over time, such as the abacus, fan, and ink, students were able to discuss invention, technologies, and progress over time and place.

By the end of the week, students participated in learning centers that brought them up to the Rancho Period in San Diego's history and integrated the information that students had learned throughout the week. They rotated between learning centers that focused on:

a. Maps: Using a large map of San Diego, students looked at the changes in maps over time. Students learned about the different ways that land is divided up and distributed, then redistributed according to events of the time. For example, students identified areas by ranchos using brand marks that identified ranchos during that period.

b. Stories: Listening to and participating in stories from the past, students handled, studied, and discussed artifacts as they listened to stories from San Diego's history. For example, listening to a story told about life on the ranchos, students passed around a tallow candle, a piece of leather, and an adobe brick.

c. Archaeology: At this excavation station, students worked with a teacher and took turns digging up artifacts from a sand pit. As they unearthed pottery shards, stone and metal tools, and other artifacts, the group analyzed each item to determine what it was, who might have used it, what it might have been used for, and how it got there. Activating analysis and interpretation skills, students were challenged to place these artifacts onto a timeline of historic eras that identified who lived in this place at what time(s) and left behind certain evidence. Students left the learning center prepared for a rich discussion about historical evidence, its limitations, and interpretive qualities of artifacts.

d. Historical Characters: As students were challenged at the beginning of the week to be on the lookout for certain people, places, and events, they revisited graphic organizers during the week to record and discuss their new information. This essential information about newcomers to San Diego and their impact on the development of the local region was determined by the content standards, teachers, and local historians. Students participated in a game of Concentration at this learning center to review this information in a variety of formats. For example, students had to find the name of a person who matched the word that described what he or she did (i.e., Ah Quin: merchant; Kate Sessions: horticulturist), or a name had to match the photograph of that person.

Using a variety of sources of information for students to observe in a museum display as well as handle in small-group learning centers, teachers facilitated the inquiry-based process of learning for students in this setting. The questions that naturally arose led students to greater exploration and understanding about evidence, reliability, and interpretation. Without this focused, hands-on experience with various forms of evidence, students are left to be passive receptors of information.

5. *The core of essential knowledge to be incorporated in the instructional program at every level must be selective enough to provide time for extended in-depth study and must be directed toward the end goals of social studies education—the development of thoughtful Americans who have the capacities for living effective personal and public lives.*

The design of School in the Park as well as the nature of museums and exhibits reflect this need for selective, in-depth studies. Third-grade students learn about animal classification, habitat survival, and physical and behavioral adaptations while at the zoo; fundamentals of art, the Silk Trade Route, and the Italian Renaissance at the art museum; and local geography, culture, and history at the historical society. Fourth-grade students learn about geography and geology in the natural history museum; archaeology and anthropology, Day of the Dead, Egypt, early humans, Navajo and Zuni cultures at the Museum of Man; photography and character education at the photographic arts museum; and teamwork, drama, and the gold rush at the theater. Fifth-grade students study aerodynamics and trajectory at the aerospace museum; chemistry, matter, energy, and weather at the science center; and ratio, percentage, and degrees at the sports museum.

Although some of these selective topics are not explicitly social studies, there remain opportunities in the program for teachers to draw connections to their social studies content. For example, third-grade students studying animal habitats at the zoo can relate these various habitats to that of the local region. Third-grade standards (California Department of Education, 2001) require students to identify geographical features of their local region and trace the ways in which people have used resources and modified the physical environment locally. The zoo itself serves as an example of how people have modified the land to create these various plant and animal habitats, as well as how San Diego's climate has been used as a resource to maintain the quality and reputation of the world-famous San Diego Zoo.

With a team of teachers at each learning site in the School in the Park program, students become accustomed to working in flexible and small groups. This requires that each student learn to work with a variety of teachers and classmates in a variety of capacities. Teamwork and team-building is an integral and consistent element throughout the program. Social participation skills are interwoven throughout the curriculum presented at every museum learning site. For example, the Junior Theater program focuses on the gold rush, but emphasizes teamwork and respect. The photographic arts museum program promotes student understanding and practice of courage, compassion, empathy, and responsibility.

Additionally, students grow accustomed to a great deal of movement within and between museums and classrooms. Common expectations for student work and behaviors are reiterated and assessed as students move into and throughout the park during the school year. These expectations are not much different from those at school and in the classroom, so students see the value of these expectations as they are upheld in a multitude of learning environments. Whereas students might otherwise adjust to different rules for different teachers, classrooms, and/or museum sites, this collaborative approach models effective cooperation among educators working together toward a common goal of educating students. The integration of character-building concepts and common expectations for work and behavior becomes guidelines for students who are empowered to lead effective personal and public lives.

As defined by the National Council for Social Studies, the primary purpose of social studies is to help young people develop the ability to make informed decisions for the public good as citizens of a culturally diverse, democratic society in an interdependent world. Empowering students to learn, think, analyze, question, interpret, and evaluate at every possible juncture, while understanding the "public good" or greater community, is carefully crafted throughout studies in the park.

Third-grade teacher James Lyons shared his thoughts about the overarching benefits of this School in the Park program while his students were immersed in interactive learning stations at the San Diego Historical Society. As students learned about ranchos, purchased items in a Chinese goods store, and analyzed artifacts after digging them up from a sand pit, Mr. Lyons explained that he grew up in San Diego and remembered coming to this public park to enjoy weekends with his family. As he returned to the park as an adult, he noticed a lack of local families coming to and using Balboa Park regularly as his family and so many other local families did years ago. "This is such a cool place and now students have access to it. The community is involved in this program and students interact with them. This lets students know that this world belongs to them—they are part of this community—and that the community shares in the responsibility of educating our children." Mr. Lyons explained that now when he comes to the park on weekends, he frequently sees students from his school who have brought their families into the park to show and teach what they have learned through this program. Mr. Lyons takes pride in seeing our youngest citizens taking ownership, pride, and care of this local treasure.

Social Studies Beyond the Classroom

Teaching and organizing the social studies curriculum can be approached in a variety of ways. Teachers might teach according to topics required at their grade level determined by national, state, or local content standards. When these standards are complex and overwhelming (for students as well as teachers), teachers might look to combine standards in a meaningful way in order to present them through topics, concepts (Parker, 1999) or themes, or Big Ideas (McTighe & Wiggins, 1998). (See Fig. 9.1.)

Teachers using the National Social Studies Standards (NCSS, 1998) might organize their curriculum around these 10 themes:

1. Culture
2. Time, Continuity, and Change
3. People, Places, and Environment
4. Individual Development and Identity
5. Individuals, Groups, and Institutions
6. Power, Authority, and Governance
7. Production, Distribution, and Consumption
8. Science, Technology, and Society

Grade	Topics	Concepts or Themes	Big Ideas
Kindergarten	Community Helpers	Communities	People work together in a community.
1st	Houses	Homes	People adapt to their environments.
2nd	Ancestors	Families	History tells the stories of people and events over time.
3rd	San Diego	Environments	Where a person lives determines how a person lives.
4th	California Gold Rush	Immigration	People move to improve their lives or because they are forced.
5th	Explorers	Exploration	Exploration leads to exchange of products, ideas, and information.
6th	Ancient China	Ancient Civilizations	All civilizations depend on leadership for survival.

FIG. 9.1. Social studies topics, concepts or themes, and big ideas.

9. Global Connections
10. Civic Ideals and Practices

If appropriate, teachers might teach according to social studies strands, primarily geography, history, economics, and civics and government. In some cases, where teaching a chronological history is not an issue, this organization makes sense, especially for young learners who are learning the foundations of social studies as geography, history, economics, and civics and government. Identifying the prominent strand in a topic-driven or chronological study of history allows teachers to also use this strand-focused approach to teaching social studies.

Organizing the social studies curriculum in any school is essential for effective planning, instruction, and assessment, especially when identifying outside resources to strengthen your classroom plans. Otherwise, teachers risk missing their social studies targets and articulating a clear purpose for social studies instruction. Once the targets are clarified (usually through content standards), the opportunities for moving the traditional classroom into the community at large are limitless. Consider some of these possibilities:

1. Community Walks: At various grade levels, students can exercise their observation, documentation, analysis, and inquiry skills by focusing on the physical and/or cultural environments within walking distance from their classroom. Communities offer opportunities to study geographic themes of place, human–environmental interaction, and movement. Maps come to life when they are integrated with the surrounding environment on or off campus. Understanding an economy can be achieved through visits to local markets, stores, community service agencies, and offices. Goods and services may be identified and categorized just as you might do with needs and wants.

2. Historical Museums: Add life to those photos, documents, and encased artifacts in museum exhibits by preparing your students before entering the museum. Tell stories, pose problem-based questions, assign roles or perspectives from which to explore information, require students to sketch, gather information, create a poem, letter, brochure, and/or news article based on information found in the exhibit. Also, use the museum and its resources to help students explore the process of historical research, archiving, and display.

3. Art Museums: Preview the museum's collection and look for exhibits that can be used to teach your period of history, topic, or theme. Portrait galleries are excellent for exploring themes of families, workers, social classes, character, jobs, contributions of people, heroes, and more. Ask museum curators if they would allow students to sit in the galleries with

clipboards and pencils to sketch portraits of each other while surrounded by excellent examples. Students should pay close attention to the details that are part of the portraits with the people: *What is the person wearing? In what setting is he or she? What colors are used? What time of day/year is this portraying? What items are integrated into the portrait? What do these things say to us?* Similar exercises may be used in looking at landscapes, still paintings, sculptures, and so on. Art makes for great discussions, interpretations, and evaluations, and is inspiring in form, color, media, and subject for student art. Replicating a period style of art, or utilizing an artist's technique or theme, can transport students to a different time, place, and way of thinking.

More Applications

With or without a coordinated program using museum and park resources, educators have multiple opportunities within their own communities to expand the four walls of their classrooms through field studies to strengthen the teaching and learning of social studies. The key to successful field studies, whether they are individual field trips, multiple rotations to one site, or a collection of trips to multiple sites, is in the planning and organization. Here is a series of questions worth consideration during this initial planning process before taking students beyond the classroom for social studies instruction, followed by an example (Table 9.1) from a third-grade teacher's perspective:

1. What are the specific goals and objectives for the students?
2. What are the core content standards that will be addressed?
3. What are some other content area standards that might be addressed?
4. Where can my students be taken to maximize teaching and learning of these standards? (Are there multiple sites?)
5. What will I do and what will my students do while we are at this site?
6. How will I prepare my students in class before we go to this learning site?
7. What will I expect (work and behaviors) from my students during the field study?
8. What will my students do in class after the field study to support and assess their learning from the field study? How will I know what they learned?
9. Who do I contact to find out more information about available dates, costs, programs, and so on?

TABLE 9.1
Preparation for Social Studies Field Trips

Questions	Considerations
What are my goals and objectives for my students?	Students will learn more about the Kumeyaay Indians, including how they worked together and used their natural environment to thrive long ago. Students will compare and contrast this to how the Kumeyaay work together and use modern technologies to live today.
What are the core content standards that will be addressed?	California History–Social Science Content Standards • 3.2: Students describe American Indian nations in their local region long ago and in the recent past. • 3.2.2: Discuss the ways in which physical geography, including climate, influenced how the local Indian nations adapted to their natural environment (e.g., how they obtained food, clothing, tools). • 3.2.4: Discuss the interaction of new settlers with the already established Indians of the region. • K–5 Chronological and Spatial Thinking: Students explain how the present is connected to the past, identifying both similarities and differences between the two, and how some things change over time and some things stay the same. • K–5 Chronological and Spatial Thinking: Students judge the significance of the relative location of a place (e.g., proximity to a harbor, on trade routes) and analyze how relative advantages or disadvantages can change over time. • K–5 Historical Interpretation: Students identify the human and physical characteristics of the places they are studying and explain how those features form the unique character of those places.
What are some other content area standards that I might be able to address?	*Science:* Earth Sciences; Investigative and Experimentation; Thinking Processes Inferring, Observing, Communicating, Comparing, Relating *Language Arts:* Reading, Writing, Speaking, Listening *Visual and Performing Arts:* Drawing, Multimedia
Where can I take my students to maximize my teaching and their learning of these standards? (Are there multiple sites?)	1. Mission Trails Regional Park 2. Barona Kumeyaay Museum 3. Museum of Man 4. Cuyamaca State Park
What will I do and what will my students do while we are at this site?	1. 1-mile park ranger-led hike through canyon and to river bed; stop along the trail to discuss and sketch plants used by Kumeyaay; grind acorns at river bed using grinding stones; listen to Kumeyaay stories at river and have small groups share stories; tour visitors' center and discuss exhibits & artifacts; meet with Kumeyaay guest; take digital pictures; students take notes along hike and bring notes back to class to use in writing assignment

(Continued)

TABLE 9.1
(Continued)

Questions	Considerations
	2. Tour museum; listen to Kumeyaay speaker in hut; analyze artifacts; focus on today's Kumeyaay; take notes to write letter to speaker about what he or she learned; take digital pictures
	3. Read selections from *Indians of the Oaks* in hut; students work in pairs to tour exhibit with clipboard to make notes and sketch artifacts; pairs co-create story titled "A Day in the Life of a Kumeyaay _____" (students determine whether they take perspective of child, woman, hunter, elder, and so on); take digital pictures
	4. Park ranger-led exploratory hike through mountain region to compare and contrast environment with canyons in Mission Trails Regional Park (Kumeyaay used both environments during different seasons); plant and animal sort and classification; listen to Kumeyaay stories and songs; students write and present story or song; art project integrating story and song and landscape; clay pottery project; visit park museum; take digital pictures
What will I do to prepare my students in class before we go to this learning site?	• KWL Chart what students know about the Kumeyaay • Read *Indian of the Oaks* with class (read aloud) • Create timelines identifying when Kumeyaay lived here, Spanish colonized, Mexico ruled, U.S. owned; major settlement periods; today • Venn diagram showing Kumeyaay long ago and Kumeyaay today • Create maps of San Diego County and identify seasonal homes of Kumeyaay; identify landforms and natural resources using relative location skills • Select lessons from *The Kumeyaay People* and *Secrets of the Trail* curriculum
What will I expect (work and behaviors) from my students during the field study?	Behaviors: • Cooperation with peers, rangers, museum educators, teachers • Collaborative work projects (small groups, pairs) • Appropriate voice levels in museums, on bus • Listening to and following directions (when to take bathroom breaks, where to go, what to do, and so on) • Respect for and careful attention to all teachers (including rangers, docents, guest speakers, peers) • Respect for cultural items, ideas, traditions, and beliefs • Positive attitudes about learning new information and from a variety of sources/environments

(Continued)

TABLE 9.1
(Continued)

Questions	Considerations
	Work:
	• On-task, focused discussions and work
	• Maximize use of flexible learning and working accommodations (on trails, sitting on ground, and the like)
	• Keen observations and records of environmental details
	• Focused on prior knowledge, information available through field studies, and creative thinking
	• Completion of projects assigned during allotted time
What will my students do in class after the field study to support and assess their learning from the field study?	• Complete writing assignments based on notes taken during field studies; use writing process
	• Share/present, analyze, discuss, and evaluate work projects
	• Reflect on learning (content and process)
	• Complete KWL Chart
	• Revisit and correct/complete Venn diagram
	• Finish reading *Indian of the Oaks* and introduce other story resources for independent reading (about other American Indian tribes)
	• Revisit maps of San Diego County and discuss effective uses and values of maps; create overlay showing today's political borders, Indian reservations, and so on
	• Create exhibit to display art projects, writing, songs
	• Develop PowerPoint slide show (multimedia presentation) using digital pictures captured throughout field studies; add reflections from students on what was learned and how it was learned
Who do I contact to find out more information about available dates, costs, programs, and the like?	• Mission Trails Regional Park Rangers
	• Barona Education Coordinator
	• Museum of Man Education Coordinator
	• Cuyamaca State Park Rangers
	• Kumeyaay Speaker's Bureau for guests
What assistance and/or other resources will I need for this field study?	• Parent drivers for Mission Trails, Barona, Museum of Man; bus for Cuyamaca
	• Cafeteria to arrange lunches for each trip
	• Parent chaperones and helpers for hikes, art, stories
What questions do I have about this field study?	• How many park rangers can I get to make hiking groups as small as possible?
	• How will clay pottery project work outdoors in Cuyamaca State Park? How will we transport wet clay back to school?
	• What should be the theme or focus of the digital slide show?

10. What assistance and/or other resources will I need for this field study?
11. What questions do I have about this field study?

In identifying learning activities to use with students during field studies, and in conjunction with cross-curricular work in the classroom, consider:

Writing. Travel logs, journals, diaries, letters, brochures, and news articles are just some of the types of primary sources that inform historians' analysis, evaluation, and interpretation of what happened in the past. As students are placed in the role of historians, they will better understand and appreciate the work of historians while engaging them in research and critical thinking about the topic, era, character, idea, and so on. While students learn through field studies, museum exploration, guest speakers, and other experiences, invite them to take notes and write about what they have learned in the form of a newspaper article, brochure, or press release. For less formal writing, ask students to use the information they have learned to share their thoughts, feelings, and opinions through diary or journal entries, letters, or travel logs. Travel logs and diaries or journals allow for continuity in recording information and thoughts as students continue to experience and learn. In this way, writing may be seen as a useful method to record, reflect, and remember—to document—rather than as a chore or skill used for the purposes of producing a project.

Geography. Using maps of local parks or attractions and integrating the teaching of directions, legends, and keys, as well as the functions and multiple uses of maps, will strengthen students' appreciation for and utilization of these important resources. To better understand the purpose and function of maps, find a place with a scenic overview for students to sit and sketch what they see. Learning that a map serves as a tool to represent what is on the land as well as relay absolute and relative locations helps students recognize the value of maps. Allow students to learn from and with maps, and engage them in mapmaking projects that are appropriate for their age levels. Dedicate a map in your classroom to tracking the places that you have taken your class through field studies.

Historians. As students learn about the roles of historians in families, organizations, and other groups, engage them in the process of recording, documenting, and assembling information gathered from your field studies. You and your students might keep portfolios, scrapbooks, travel logs, or diaries—physically or digitally—to record information and organize the information in a meaningful manner. Visit and revisit the class (or individual) records regularly to address issues of perspective, time, context, and so on. Look for what the records tell and do not tell. Find opportunities for students to share their records with their families, guests to the classroom, and others. Connect these records to other public records, including the newspaper, legal records, and oral histories.

Reading. Select literature that will enhance students' visual imagery and their understanding of people from a different era, or give multiple perspectives on an event, and use stories during field studies or to prepare students in the classroom before field studies. Sometimes, a story such as *The True Story of the Three Little Pigs* will highlight the importance of considering the missing voices on an historic event portrayed in an exhibit or monument. *Right Here on the Spot* or *The House on Maple Street* helps students consider the evidence of the past that lies beneath the Earth's surface when visiting any particular place to consider who lived there, what happened there, and how things have changed over time. Folktales, legends, and cultural tales are excellent sources to enhance students' understandings and appreciation of people over place and time. Many offer students opportunities to connect stories, storylines, and/or characters across regions of the world and to better understand periods of exploration and exchange.

Conclusion

Social studies should be fun, interactive, meaningful, and memorable. Most adults will recall learning social studies through field-based experiences more than through typical classroom exercises. Students are the first to tell us that learning social studies is fun and exciting when they get to go places, imagine travels, dress up in costumes, taste foods, dig up artifacts, play games, and figure things out with their friends. Understanding that our job entails more than making school "fun" for students, it will benefit our teaching and learning community to pay attention to how students prefer to learn, then plan for engaging lessons inside and outside of the classroom, and ultimately help our students succeed in achieving curricular goals and standards.

REFERENCES

California Department of Education. (2001). *History–social science framework for California's public schools.* Sacramento, CA: Author.

McTighe, J., & Wiggins, G. (1998). *Understanding by design.* Alexandria, VA: Association for Supervision and Curriculum Development.

National Council for the Social Studies. (1989). *Charting a course: Social studies for the 21st century.* Washington, DC: The National Commission on the Social Studies in the Schools.
National Council for the Social Studies. (1998). *National social studies content standards.* Washington, DC: Author.
Parker, W. (1999). *Adventures in time and place.* New York: Macmillan McGraw-Hill.
Pigdon, K., & Woolley, M. (1993). *The big picture: Integrating children's learning.* Portsmouth, NH: Heinemann.
Steffey, S., & Hood, W. (1994). *If this is social studies, why isn't it boring?* York, ME: Stenhouse.

RESOURCES

Addy, S. H. (1991). *Right here on this spot.* New York: Houghton Mifflin.
Gilchrist, C. (1999). *Stories from the Silk Road.* New York: Barefoot Books.
Labastida, R., & Caldeira, D. (1998). *The Kumeyaay people.* San Diego, CA: San Diego County Office of Education.
Labastida, R., & Caldeira, D. (1999). *Secrets of the trail.* San Diego, CA: San Diego County Office of Education.
Lee, M. (1978). *Indian of the oaks.* New York: Acoma Books.
O'Neill, M. (1990). *Hailstones and halibut bones.* New York: Doubleday.
Pryor, B. (1992). *The house on Maple Street.* New York: HarperTrophy.
Scieszka, J. (1997). *The true story of the three little pigs.* New York: Puffin.

About the Editors

Ian Pumpian, PhD, is Professor of Educational Leadership at San Diego State University and Executive Director of the City Heights Educational Collaborative. He earned his doctorate from the University of Wisconsin–Madison in 1980. His special committee degree included an emphasis in educational administration, curriculum instruction, and personnel preparation for special populations as well as legal and medical issues pertaining to school and special populations. Ian Pumpian has been a faculty member at San Diego State University since 1981. During that time he has been a coordinator of teacher credential programs in the area of severe disabilities, the chairperson of the Department of Special Education, and a faculty member in the Department of Administration, Rehabilitation, and Postsecondary Education. As a full professor from the Department of Administration, Rehabilitation, and Postsecondary Education, he has been responsible for educational leadership master's programs and the development of a new EdD program. For the past seven years, Dr. Pumpian has assumed an administrative position in the office of the president of San Diego State University. His role is the Executive Director of the City Heights Educational Collaborative. The City Heights Educational Collaborative involves three inner-city public schools within the area of City Heights, a designated federal Enterprise Community that has historically been characterized by high levels of poverty. At most of the schools in the City Heights area, 30 different languages are spoken and the students represent traditionally underrepresented groups based on notions of race, national origin, gender, age, and disability. The purpose of the Collaborative is to create for the University the educational equivalent of a teaching hospital in the schools and at the same time create an articulated K to 16 program and partnership. Although the three public schools are part of the San Diego Unified School District, San Diego State University has assumed district-level responsibility for the school and Dr. Pumpian serves as the off-site administrator, supervisor, and instructional leader for the schools.

Douglas Fisher, PhD, is a Professor in the Department of Teacher Education at San Diego State University and the Director of Professional Development for the City Heights Educational Collaborative. He is the recipient of an International Reading Association Celebrate Literacy Award as well as a Christa McAuliffe award for excellence in teacher education. He has published numerous articles on reading and literacy, differentiated instruction, and curriculum design as well as books, such as *Improving Adolescent Literacy: Strategies at Work* and *Responsive Curriculum Design in Secondary Schools: Meeting the Diverse Needs of Students*. He has taught a variety of courses in SDSU's teacher-credentialing program as well as graduate-level courses on English language development and literacy. He has also taught classes in English, writing, and literacy development to secondary school students.

Susan Wachowiak, MA, is the designer and Director of School in the Park. Her educational career has seen her as a teacher in elementary and middle schools, a resource teacher, and district curriculum writer in language arts, science, social studies, math, and race/human relations. She was a team member in the national science reform effort sponsored by the American Association for the Advancement of Science, Project 2062, and a contributor to the book, *Benchmarks for Science Literacy*. She has been a school administrator for 14 years during which time she has created and worked in off-site programs for elementary school students.

About the Authors

Maria Grant, EdD, has been working as a classroom teacher for over 19 years. She conducted research related to museum education as part of her doctoral degree. She teaches physics at Hoover High School, a part of the City-Heights/SDSU Educational Collaborative, where she has worked with professional development for high school teachers with a focus on literacy integration. Maria is currently a member of the Glencoe California Advisory Board for the adoption of science texts, and has authored literacy strategies for the Florida State science textbook adoption. In addition, Maria co-authored an article about the integration of information literacy in a doctoral program using the standards set forth by the Association of College and Research Libraries. Maria has worked to help develop assessment strategies designed to evaluate educational software and has collaborated on the development of companion teacher guides to support use of science software. She has worked as Curriculum Coordinator for the Science Enrichment Program (SEP) at San Diego State University where she also teaches science methodology for preservice elementary school teachers. Maria has participated as a consultant to the State Boards of Education on a study project examining earthquake safety in the schools, and continues to explore her great interest in supporting young people in developing an interest and understanding of science curriculum.

Nancy Farnan, PhD, has spent her life in classrooms, as a classroom teacher, reading specialist, and university professor. She works with children and adolescents in elementary and middle schools, and in secondary classrooms; with adults in teacher preparation; and with graduate students in master's and doctoral programs. Currently, she is a Professor in the College of Education at San Diego State University and Director of the School of Teacher Education. At the university, she has taught courses in reading, writing, literature, middle-level education, and research processes. Dr. Farnan has worked with the California Literature Project; speaks regularly at state and national conferences; serves on several editorial review boards; and publishes her work in such periodicals as *Reading and Writing Quarterly*, *Journal of Reading*, and *The New Advocate*. Her books include *Writing Effectively: Helping Children Master the Conventions of Writing*, co-authored with Leif Fearn (Allyn & Bacon, 1998); *Children's Writing: Perspectives from Research*, co-authored with Karin Dahl (International Reading Association, 1998); and *Interactions: Teaching Writing and the Language Arts*, co-authored with Dr. Fearn (Houghton Mifflin, 2001).

Leif Fearn teaches literacy and social studies at San Diego State University. His work in community schools reaches back to 1965 when, as an employee of the Navajo Tribe, he worked in tribal education. He writes both long and short fiction as well as nonfiction and meets weekly with a writers' group to lie, swear, drink, and talk about writing.

James Flood, PhD, Distinguished Research Professor of Language and Literacy at San Diego State University has taught in preschool, elementary, and secondary schools and has been a language arts supervisor and vice principal. He has also been a Fulbright scholar at the University of Lisbon in Portugal and the President of the National Reading Conference. James Flood has chaired and co-chaired many IRA, NCTE, NCRE, and NRC committees. Currently Dr. Flood teaches graduate courses at SDSU. He has co-authored and edited many articles, columns, texts, handbooks, and children's materials on reading and language arts issues. Two of his recent books are *Content Area Reading and Learning*, which is in its second edition, and *The Handbook of Research on Teaching Literacy Through the Communicative and Visual Arts*. His many educational awards include being named as the Outstanding Teacher Educator in the Department of Teacher Education at SDSU, the Distinguished Research Lecturer from SDSU's Graduate Division of Research, and selection as a member of both California's and IRA's Reading Hall of Fame. Dr. Flood is also a co-editor of *The California Reader* and a member of the board of directors of the International Reading Association.

Nancy Frey, PhD, is Associate Professor of Literacy in the School of Teacher Education at San Diego State University and the Coordinator of

Professional Development Schools for the City Heights Educational Collaborative. She is a recipient of the Christa McAuliffe award for excellence in teacher education. She has published numerous articles on reading and literacy, assessment, intervention, and curriculum design as well as books, such as *Language Arts Workshop: Purposeful Reading and Writing Instruction*, co-authored with Doug Fisher and published by Merrill Prentice Hall. She teaches a variety of courses in SDSU's teacher-credentialing program on elementary reading and language arts and on supporting students with diverse learning needs.

Diane Lapp, EdD, Distinguished Research Professor of Language and Literacy in the Department of Teacher Education at San Diego State University, has taught in elementary and middle schools. Her major areas of research and instruction have been of issues related to struggling readers and their families who live in urban settings. Dr. Lapp, who directs and teaches field-based preservice and graduate programs and courses, continues to team teach in public school classrooms. Diane Lapp has co-authored and edited many articles, columns, texts, handbooks, and children's materials on reading and language arts issues. Two of her recent books are *Teaching Reading to Every Child*, a reading methods textbook in its fourth edition, and *The Handbook of Research in Teaching the English Language Arts*, now in its second edition. She has also chaired and co-chaired several IRA and NRC committees. She is currently the co-chair of IRA's Early Literacy Commission. Her many educational awards include being named as the Outstanding Teacher Educator and Faculty Member in the Department of Teacher Education at SDSU, the Distinguished Research Lecturer from SDSU's Graduate Division of Research, a member of the California Reading Hall of Fame, and IRA's 1996 Outstanding Teacher Educator of the Year. Dr. Lapp is the co-editor of California's literacy journal, *The California Reader*.

Kate Masarki, PhD, has been involved in mathematics education involving students and teachers for over 30 years. One of her passions is to help students, teachers, and the person on the street the mathematics that surrounds them and adds to the richness of their lives. A former algebra teacher, Kate is currently an Assistant Professor at San Diego State University.

Nan L. McDonald, EdD, is currently Associate Professor and Coordinator of Music Education at San Diego State University's School of Music and Dance. With over 30 years of teaching experience in preschool through K to University Level Music Education, Integrated Arts for Classroom Teachers, Music and Early Literacy Development, and Classroom Discipline and Management, she is actively involved in the education of future arts specialists and classroom teachers. Dr. McDonald leads ongoing Integrated Arts and English Language Development professional growth for teachers within three underserved, urban schools within the City Heights/ SDSU Educational Collaborative Schools (Rosa Parks Elementary School, Monroe Clark Middle School, Hoover High School). There she is the Director of K to 12 Integrated Arts Curriculum. She is the author of numerous articles in national and international arts education publications, a Program Author for Scott Foresman/Silver Burdett Music K to 8 national text series in music (2002 and 2005 editions of "Making Music"), and has co-authored two books about Arts Integration and Literacy Instruction (Scarecrow, 2002, and Guilford, 2005).

In addition to her writing and teaching background, she has co-created and performed professionally in over 300 performances of "Literature Alive," a music, dance, and drama performance series to promote reading in the elementary school. She has recently served for two consecutive terms as the Executive State Vice President of the California Music Educators Association and continues to collaborate with several school districts and universities nationwide in professional growth offerings for practicing arts specialists and classroom teachers.

Donna Ross, PhD, is an Associate Professor of Science in the School of Teacher Education at San Diego State University. She teaches a variety of courses focusing on science methods for prospective teachers, science for English Learners, and integrating science and literacy. She has published numerous articles on increasing and improving science education in elementary schools. She directs a program in which she teams science graduate students with elementary teachers for periods of 16 weeks of science instruction and she coordinates another program to provide extended science field experiences to urban youth. Prior to her work at the university, Donna was an elementary school teacher and a wetlands ecologist.

Emily M. Schell, EdD, is a Visiting Professor at San Diego State University and the Social Studies Education Director for the City Heights Educational Collaborative. In addition to teaching Social Studies Methods to teacher candidates and supervising student teachers, she provides professional development for teachers in the areas of standards, assessment, and curriculum development. While a teacher for San Diego Unified Schools, she always embraced opportunities to extend the confines of her classroom and inspire learning through field studies.

Author Index

Note: Page numbers in *italics* indicate reference pages.

A

Adams, M. J., 30, *40*
Adamson, S., 31, *42*
Addy, S. H., *145*
Aliki, _, *58*
Allen, J., *58*
Allington, R., 35, *42*
Almasi, J., 40, *40*
Alvermann, D. E., 25, *28*, 40, *41*, 52, *58*
Armbruster, B. B., 44, *58*
Armstrong, T., 15, *27*

B

Baker, K., 35, *42*
Bakhtin, M. M., 30, *40*
Barnes, D., 35, *41*
Baylor, B., 56, *58*
Bear, D. R., 45, *58*
Biancarosa, G., 45, *58*
Block, C., 34, 35, *41, 42*
Booth, D., 38, *41*
Boothby, P. R., 52, *58*
Bourdieu, P., 25–26, *27*
Broaddus, K., *58*

Brooks, G., 35, *42*
Brooks, J. G., 15, *27*
Brooks, M. G., 15, *27*
Brown, A. L., 52, *58, 59*
Bruner, J., 31, *41*
Bruner, J. S., *41*
Burns, M. S., 44, *59*
Burz, H. L., 85, *94*

C

Caldeira, D., *145*
California County Superintendent Educational Services Association, 71, 77
California Department of Education, 71, 77, 83, 84, *94*, 135, *144*
Campione, J. C., 52, *58*
Carger, C. L., 37, *41*
Carlson, S., 20, *27*
Chaney, C., 30, *41*
Chiola-Nakai, D., 31, *42*
Chomsky, N. A., 30, *41*
Christie, F., 30, *41*
Clark, R. C., 11, *14*
Clay, M. M., 30, *41*
Coker, D., 45, *58*

153

Crawford, K., 33, *42*
Cronin, J., 35, *42*
Csikszentmihalyi, I. S., *27*
Csikszentmihalyi, M., 16, 17, 21, 24, *27*, *28*
Curriculum and Instruction Steering Committee of National Center for History in the Schools, 62, 71, 77
Curriculum Development and Supplemental Materials Commissions, 98, 106, *108*

D

Daane, M., 63, 77
Daniels, H., *58*
Deffes, R., 45, *58*
Dierking, L. D., 17, *27*, 109, 121–122, *122*
Dodge, B., 57, *58*

E, F

Emig, J., 62, 77
Falk, J. H., 17, *27*, 109, 121–122, *122*
Farnan, N., 45, *58*, 62, 63, 66, 72, 77
Fearn, L., 45, *58*, 62, 63, 66, 72, 77
Fielding, L., 45, *59*
Fisher, D., 40, *41*, 45, *58*, 84, *95*
Flood, J., 30, 40, *41*, *42*, *58*, 84, *95*
Fountas, I. C., *58*
Freire, P., 46, *58*
Frey, N., 45, *58*

G

Gardner, H., 15, 17, *27*
Gilchrist, C., 125, *145*
Griffin, P., 44, *59*
Grotzer, T. A., 26, *27*
Grove, K., 25–26, *27*
Guthrie, J., 40, *41*

H

Halliday, M. A. K., 31, *41*
Hancock, M., 84, *94*
Harris, T. L., 44, *58*
Hatch, E., 36, *41*

Heffernan, L., 31, *42*
Hein, G. E., 18, *27*
Hektner, J., 24, *28*
Hermanson, K., 17, *27*
Hodges, R. E., 44, *58*
Holdaway, D., *58*
Hood, W., 128, *145*
Hooper-Greenhill, E., 8, *14*, 18, *27*
Hurt, N., 34, *41*

I

Invernizzi, M., 45, *58*
Ivey, G., *58*

J

Jacobs, H. H., 15, 19, *28*, 84, *95*
Jaggar, A. M., 31, *41*
Jensen, E., 84, *94*
Jin, Y., 63, 77
Johnston, F., 45, *58*
Juel, C., 45, *58*

K

Kahn, L. H., 33, 37, *42*
Kamil, M. L., 44, *59*
Kaser, S., 33, *42*
Kauffman, G., 33, 37, *42*
Keene, E. O., 56, *59*
Knapp, M., 36, *41*

L

Labastida, R., *145*
Lapp, D., 40, *41*, *58*, 84, *95*
Lee, M. H., 54, *58*, *145*
Lindfors, J., 36, *41*
Lonigan, C., 30, 31, *42*

M

Macedo, D. P., 46, *58*
Maloch, B., 31, *41*
Marshall, K., 85, *94*
Marzano, R. J., 15, 25, *28*

AUTHOR INDEX

Mayer, R. E., 11, *14*
McCormack, R. L., 31, *41*
McDonald, N., 84, *95*
McKeown, M., 40, *40*
McTighe, J., 15, *28*, 137, *144*
Mid-Continent Regional Education Laboratory, *59*
Moore, K., 40, *41*
Morrow, L., 35, *42*
Muise, M., 31, *42*
Music Educators National Conference, *95*

N

National Board of Professional Teaching Standards, *59*
National Commission on Writing in America's Schools and Colleges, 63, *77*
National Council for the Social Studies, 137, *145*
National Council of Teachers of Mathematics, 106, *108*
National Research Council, 112, *122*
Nelson, E., 35, *42*
Nieto, S., 7, *14*, 25, *28*

O

Oakar, M., 34, *41*
Ogle, D. M., 52, 54, *59*
O'Neill, M., 126, *145*
Osborn, J. H., 44, *58*

P

Padak, N., 36, *41*
Palincsar, A. S., 52, *59*
Paratore, J. R., 31, *41*
Paris, S. G., 51, *59*
Parker, W., 137, *145*
Passeron, J. C., 26, *27*
Payne, R., 25, *28*
Pearson, P. D., 45, *59*
Perksy, H., 63, *77*
Pickering, D., 15, *28*
Pigdon, K., 127, *145*
Pilgreen, J., *59*
Pinnell, G. S., 31, *41*, *58*
Platt, N. G., 36, *41*

Prentiss, T., 40, *41*
Pressley, M., 35, *42*
Pryor, B., *145*
Putnam, L. R., 31, *42*

R

Reinking, D., 40, *42*
Roschelle, J., 12, *14*
Rosenblatt, L. M., 44, 48–49, *59*, 84, *95*

S

Sage, S., 15, *28*
Salus, _, 30, *42*
Samuels, J., 44, *59*
Satir, V., 40, *42*
Scieszka, J., *145*
Searfoss, L. W., 31, *42*
Semper, R. J., 13, 14, *14*, 17, 24, *28*
Shear, J., 31, *42*
Short, K. G., 33, 37, *42*
Silliman, E., 31, *42*
Sizer, T. R., 12, *14*
Snow, C. E., 44, *59*
Spandel, V., 72, *77*
Spencer, S., 45, *59*
Stanovich, K. E., *59*
Stauffer, R. G., 52, 54, *59*
Steen, L. A., *108*
Steffey, S., 128, *145*
Sticht, T., 46, *59*
Stiggins, R. J., 72, *77*
Strickland, D. S., 25, *28*
Sulzby, E., 30, *42*

T

Teale, W., 30, *42*
Templeton, S., 45, *58*
Tomlinson, C. A., 15, *28*
Torp, L., 15, *28*
Tracey, D., 35, *42*
Turner, J. C., 51, *59*

V

Vasquez, V., 31, *42*
Vygotsky, L., 30, *42*, 84, *95*

W

Wallach, G., 38, *42*
Wasik, B. A., 51, *59*
Wells, G., 30, 31, *42*
Wharton-McDonald, R., 35, *42*
Whitehurst, G., 30, 31, *42*
Wiggins, G., 137, *144*

Wilkinson, I., 31, *42*
Woo, D., 35, *42*
Woolley, M., 127, *145*

Z

Zimmerman, S., 56, *59*

Subject Index

Note: Page numbers in *italic* indicate figures; those in **boldface** indicate tables.

A

Academic Performance Index (API), 7–8
Academic standards. *See* Formal/informal learning blend; Standards-based curriculum
Aerospace Museum
  interdisciplinary instruction in, 13
  mathematics in, 104
  oral language development in, 37
  science instruction in, 115
API, 7–8
Archeological dig activity, 99–101
Arts
  integrating in curriculum, 91–93
  in museum classrooms
    Junior Theater, 88–89
    Museum of Art, 79–83
    Museum of Photographic Arts, 89–91
    San Diego Historical Society Museum, 85–86
    San Diego Zoo, 87–88
  in reading instruction, 49–51, *51*
  standards for, 83–85
Assessment
  as challenge, 11
  of classroom language environment, 31–32
  of writing, 72–74
Authentic learning. *See* Formal/informal learning blend

B

Baseball. *See* Hall of Champions Museum
Biological adaptation unit, 47–48, *48*

C

City Heights community, 5
City Heights Educational Collaborative, 4
Classroom space, 11
Commerce game, 33–34
Community, in social studies goals, 136
Community walks, 138
Critical thinking, 130–132
Cultural capital, 25–26
Curiosity
  in literacy-rich environments, 20–24
  science instruction and, 120–121

Curriculum. *See* Standards-based curriculum
Curriculum maps, 18–20

D

Deep understanding, 26–27
Drama. *See* Junior Theater

E

Engaged learning
  in oral language development, 39–40
  in science, 111–112
  writing as, 65–66, 77
English language learners
  arts and, 84
  vocabulary development in, 115
  writing instruction and, 74
Enjoyment, 24
Equal opportunity, 117

F

Fantasy Baseball. *See* Hall of Champions Museum
Field trips
  versus School in the Park, 2–4, *2*
  in social studies
    learning activities for, 143–144
    preparing for, 139–143, **140–142**
"Flow," 16–17, 24–25
Formal/informal learning blend
  cultural capital in, 25–26
  curriculum maps in, 18–20
  described, 8, 18
  literacy-rich environments in, 20–25
Future, social studies and, 128–130

G

Geography, 143
Gold Rush study
  drama in, 88–89
  oral language development in, 36–37
  social studies in, 130–132

H

Habits of mind, 12
Hall of Champions Museum
  interdisciplinary instruction in, 14
  literacy-richness in, 24
  mathematics in, 105–106
  oral language development in, 38
History. *See also* San Diego Historical Society Museum
  as learning activity, 143–144
  of School in the Park, 4

I

IMAX theater, 12
In-depth studies, 135
Informal learning. *See* Formal/informal learning
Inquiry, in reading instruction
  in artistic unit, 50
  in biological adaptation unit, 47–48
  described, 46
  in historical unit, 53
Inquiry-based science, 121
Instructional design, 8–9
Interdisciplinary instruction
  benefits of, 11–14
  in curriculum maps, 20
  in science, 116–117
  in social studies, 127–128
"In the zone," 16–17

J

Junior Theater
  arts in, 88–89
  oral language development in, 36–37

K

Key standards, 18–19
Kumeyaay study
  arts in, 85–86
  reading instruction in, 52–55, *53, 55*

SUBJECT INDEX

L

Learning centers, for social studies, 132–135
Learning materials, for social studies, 132–135
Lifelong learning, 117
Literacy interactions, 74–76
Literacy-rich environments, 20–25

M

Mathematics instruction
  contextualization of, 98–99
  described, 97–98
  implementing, 108
  lesson planning for, 106–107
  in museum classrooms
    Aerospace Museum, 104
    archeological dig activity, 99–101
    Hall of Champions Museum, 105–106
    Museum of Art, 102–103
    San Diego Zoo, 101–102
Media, for social studies, 132–135
Mosaic tile activity, 33
Museum of Art
  arts in, 79–83
  interdisciplinary instruction in, 13
  literacy-richness in, 21
  mathematics in, 102–103
  oral language development in, 32–34
  reading instruction in, 49–51, *51*
  social studies in, 124–125
Museum of Man
  interdisciplinary instruction in, 12
  oral language development in, 35–36
  science instruction in, 114
Museum of Photographic Arts
  literacy-richness in, 22–23
  visual arts in, 89–91
Museums
  learning potential in, 17
  School in the Park impact on, 10–11, *110*
  as social studies resource, 138–139

O

Oral language development
  assessing in classrooms, 31–32
  engaged learning in, 39–40
  language functions in, 31
  in museum classrooms
    Aerospace Museum, 37
    Hall of Champions Museum, 38
    Historical Society Museum, 34–35
    Junior Theater, 36–37
    Museum of Art, 32–34
    Museum of Man, 35–36
    San Diego Zoo, 38–39
  social interaction in, 30–31
  writing and, 75–76

P

Parent involvement, 10
Perception, in reading instruction
  in artistic unit, 49–50
  in biological adaptation unit, 47
  described, 46
  in historical unit, 52–53
Photography. *See* Museum of Photographic Arts
Price Charities, 4
Prior knowledge
  cultural capital and, 25–26
  science instruction and, 114
Professional development, 9–10
Program description, 5–6

R

Reading instruction
  in classroom versus museum setting, 45–46, *45*
  implementing with time constraints, 55–57
  in literacy development, 44
  reader response in, 48–49
  reading strategies in, 51–52
  reading the world in
    artistic unit, 49–51, *51*
    biological unit, 47–48, *48*
    described, 46
    historical unit, 52–55, *53, 55*
  in social studies, 144
  standards for, 44
Reflection, in reading instruction
  in artistic unit, 50–51
  in biological adaptation unit, 48
  described, 46
  in historical unit, 53–54

Relevance, 24
Reuben H. Fleet Science Center
  impact of School in the Park on, *110*
  interdisciplinary instruction in, 12
  literacy-richness in, 23
  science instruction in, 111–112, 118–121

S

San Diego Historical Society Museum
  arts in, 85–86
  interdisciplinary instruction in, 13
  literacy-richness in, 24
  oral language development in, 34–35
  reading instruction in, 52–55, *53, 55*
San Diego Zoo
  arts in, 87–88
  literacy-richness in, 21–22
  mathematics in, 101–102
  oral language development in, 38–39
  reading instruction in, 47–48, *48*
School in the Park
  described, 5–6
  as equal opportunity, 117
  versus field trips, 2–4, *2*
  history of, 4
  impact on museums, 10–11, *110*
  interdisciplinary instruction in, 11–14
  organization and structure of, 8–10
  students served by, 6–8
Science instruction
  approaches to, 113–115
  curiosity and, 120–121
  interdisciplinary instruction in, 116–117
  in museum classrooms
    Aerospace Museum, 115
    Museum of Man, 114
    Reuben H. Fleet Science Center, 111–112, 118–121
    teacher benefits of, 117–118
  standards for, 112–113
  vocabulary development in, 115–116
Selective studies, 135
Self-questioning, in reading instruction, 52
Silk Road study
  arts in, 79–83
  mathematics in, 102–103
  social studies in, 123–127
  writing instruction in, 66–71

Social interaction, in oral language development, 30–31
Social studies
  field studies in
    learning activities for, 143–144
    preparing for, 139–143, **140–142**
  organizing curriculum for, 137–138, *137*
  outside resources for, 138–139
  in Silk Road study, 123–127
  Task Force goals for, 127–137
Standards-based curriculum
  arts in, 83–85
  curriculum maps and, 18–20
  for reading instruction, 44
  at School in the Park, 7
  for science instruction, 112–113
Stereotypes, of scientists, 114–115
Student population, 6–8

T

Task Force of the National Commission on the Social Studies, 127
Teacher expectations, 9, 136
Teamwork, 135–136

V

Vocabulary development
  in reading instruction, 52–53
  in science instruction, 115–116

W

Walks, as social studies resource, 138
WebQuests, 57
Writing instruction
  engaged learning in, 65–66, 77
  intentional, 63–65, 76–77
  literacy interactions in, 74–75
  oral foundations of, 75–76
  process approach to, 62–63
  in Silk Road study, 66–71
  in social studies, 143
  writing assessment and, 72–74
  writing curriculum for, 74

CPSIA information can be obtained at www.ICGtesting.com
Printed in the USA
BVOW011201161011

273744BV00006B/23/P